Bienvenidos to Our Kitchen

AUTHENTIC MEXICAN COOKING

Bienvenidos to Our Kitchen

AUTHENTIC MEXICAN COOKING

Luis and Marilyn Peinado

PELICAN PUBLISHING COMPANY
Gretna 1992

The word "Pelican" and the depiction of a pelican are trademarks of Pelican Publishing Company, Inc., and are registered in the U.S. Patent and Trademark Office.

Library of Congress Cataloging-in-Publication Data

Peinado, Luis.
    Bienvenidos to our kitchen : authentic Mexican cooking / Luis and
Marilyn Peinado.
      p.   cm.
    Includes index.
    ISBN 0-88289-873-6
    1. Cookery, Mexican.   I. Peinado, Marilyn.   II. Title.
TX716.M4P45   1992
641.5972—dc20   91-42877
                                                                CIP

Manufactured in Hong Kong

Published by Pelican Publishing Company, Inc.
1101 Monroe Street, Gretna, Louisiana 70053

To the late Marcelina Peña Vda. de Juarez,
in memory of the many years
we spent together in the kitchen

Contents

Acknowledgments

Thanks to my husband and coauthor, Luis, who joined into this project with the same enthusiasm he has always shown for all things Latin American and made what could have become a chore a most exciting and memorable experience.

Gracias to our friends in Mexico who took so much interest in this book, in particular architect Rubén Gaytan and my father, H. V. Lemley, who took time from their busy schedules running the Tlapaneco Mission, Inc. to take photographs.

Thanks to Luis's favorite former student in English, Señor Antonio Ariza Cañadilla, general manager of Industrias Vinícolas Pedro Domecq, S.A. de C.V., who assisted with the photography. We were proud to have the interest of Lic. Enrique Figueroa, director of public relations of Industrias Vinicolas Pedro Domecq, S.A. de C.V., and organizer of the First World Congress of Gastronomy in Mexico City in 1989, in organizing some of the photography for us.

We wish to give special thanks for the courtesy of María Orsini, who shared some of the photographs she dedicated at the 1990 World Congress of Gastronomy in Mexico City.

Introduction

This cookbook is an honest endeavor to compile all of our Mexican home-cooking recipes. Each recipe has been individually tested in our kitchen many times. I was born and raised in Mexico and my husband and coauthor, Luis, has lived for more than twenty years in Mexico. It is our sincere hope that this cookbook will serve the North Americans and especially the Latin Americans who have had to emigrate and are homesick for their Mexican cooking. It is also a reliable reference for people who still live in Mexico. Whether you live north or south of the Mexican borders, or overseas, if you have visited Mexico for one reason or another and would like to partake of Mexican cuisine, this is the cookbook for you.

My parents, the Lemleys, were invited to Mexico in 1938 by President Lazaro Cardenas to work with the indigenous people as missionaries. My father took out a map of the Republic of Mexico and chose to work in the most remote village that existed in the Sierra Mountains of Guerrero: Tlacoapa. My parents founded the Tlapaneco Mission, Inc. in 1938. They had a dream of adopting and educating as many Tlapaneco youngsters as their resources would permit so that they in turn would return to help the Tlapaneco people. The mission required both my mother and father to travel a great part of the year.

Many Tlapaneco boys and girls lived in my home as I grew up in Cuernavaca, Morelos. Needless to say, meals had to be regional and plentiful. Marcelina Peña Vda. de Juarez, ''Marcy'' as she was called, was in charge of running the house and she was an excellent cook. Marcy was the widow of Leonardo, a revolutionary soldier in the Mexican Revolution of 1910-20. I will always cherish the countless hours we spent together in the kitchen, where she not only trained me to make regional dishes but also spoke frequently of her marriage to Leonardo and how she carefully prepared his meals and took them to him wherever he was at mealtime, including the battlefront.

There were also many parties organized at my home in Cuernavaca where Mexican delicacies were served. I used to help prepare these feasts. I had more fun preparing the food than attending the parties. The first time I worked in the kitchen I needed a stool because I was not tall enough to reach the stove.

Luis left his native La Paz, Bolivia in 1958 and headed for the University of Wisconsin. While he was studying in Wisconsin, he met his first wife, who was from Mexico. He moved to Mexico City, where he lived for more than twenty years. At first, he gave English classes to prominent businessmen, professionals, and government officials, who to this day refer to Luis as "Professor." One day, encouraged by a former student, Luis entered the real estate business. Luis enjoyed selling real estate because he had a chance to travel to the neighboring states and to the states along the Pacific Coast. He began to cherish the grilled shrimp served in little shacks along the Coast of Manzanillo and the albóndigas (meatballs) with chipotle sauce served in Yautepec, Morelos. Soon he was cooking these delicacies at home for his family.

The word of Luis's seasoned fingers quickly spread among the Mexican folks. People in Mexico City began to request him to cook for their special events and parties. Everyone began to ask him for recipes. His most popular recipe among the Mexicans are his marinated chilies. It takes a Fort Knox to keep the Mexican public out of his pickled chilies while they are still curing.

Luis and I got married in 1982, and we decided to write this cookbook together in 1988. It has been written on weekends and when we could spare the time, but it has been fun. Although primarily intended to give others pleasure, we also find it useful to have our recipes down on paper for us to use as well. Without Luis's contribution, this would not be the excellent cookbook it now is.

Enjoy these recipes. Rest assured that this is what is really eaten in Mexico; this is what you would be served if you were invited to a Mexican family's home.

MARILYN PEINADO
San Antonio, Texas

PART I
FOUNDATIONS OF MEXICAN COOKING

CHAPTER 1
CORN

Corn, beans, and chilies are the basics of the Mexican diet. Whatever else they may serve, the indigenous people of Mexico always count on these three fundamental elements.

The Spanish conquistadors learned that the Aztec and Mayan civilizations were knowledgeable about farming many plants that were unknown in Europe. The major agricultural find in the New World was the venerated corn. Chronicles depict corn as prehistoric. Archaeologists found artifacts, hieroglyphics, and what have you with corn depicted as having religious significance.

Hernan Cortez might have found only wandering inhabitants in Mexico instead of the great Aztec and Mayan civilizations were it not for their farming knowledge. And the same would be the case of Francisco Pizarro in his conquest of the ''Tahuantisuyo'' Empire of the Inca Civilization, stretching from what are now known as the South American Republics of Colombia, Ecuador, Peru, Bolivia, and the northern parts of Chile and Argentina. The Portuguese explorer, Alvarez Cabral, in the conquest of Brazil, also found corn as a basic staple in the numerous tribes that he found. In other words, the whole American continent consumed corn in pre-Columbian times.

The newly discovered corn was loaded on ships that returned to Spain and consequently it disseminated in Europe. Conversely, wheat to be cultivated in the American continent was loaded on ships that sailed from Spain. In this way the New World was exposed to wheat.

The Aztecs, the Mayans, and other more minor civilizations of Central America would use the corn to make ''tortillas,'' which became their ''bread'' and one of the most important staples of their daily diet. In order to make the tortillas it was necessary to have a dough, and so they created *nixtamal,* the basic element of the tortilla.

Preparation of the Nixtamal: Dried corn kernels are heated in a mildly corrosive solution of water and lime (calcium oxide) until the kernel skins are soft. After standing for one day, the kernels are skinned. The skinless kernels are called *nixtamal*, an Aztec word still in use. Nixtamal is the single most important element in Mexican cooking. The most common use of nixtamal is to mash the soaked kernels into masa. When they are not mashed they are used as hominy.

Preparation of the Masa—Old Method: Women used to put some of the nixtamal on a flat volcanic stone known as a *metate*. Then using a stone rolling pin, called a *metlalpil,* they would crush the nixtamal until it became the dough called *masa*. The metate is a relic of the past.

Preparation of the Masa—Modern Method: Those who grow their own corn take the nixtamal to the tortilleria for grinding. But Mexican cooks just prefer to buy ready-ground masa from a tortilleria for home-cooking purposes.

Hand-Made Tortillas—Old Method: A woman first heated her comal (griddle) barbecue style. She then wet her hands in a bowl of water, pinched a piece of masa and shaped a small ball, and covered the remaining masa to keep it from drying. With clapping movements she acrobatically flattened it into a flat round dough, somewhere between six to eight inches in diameter.

Hand-Made Tortillas—Modern Method: The comal is heated. Two pieces of wax paper or cellophane are placed between the two round presses of the special tortilla press. Hands are dipped in a bowl of water before pinching a piece of masa to shape a small ball, and the remaining masa is covered to keep moist. The ball is flattened between the tortilla press. Paper or cellophane is removed from the flat round dough.

The Cooking of Home-Made Tortillas—Old and Modern Methods: The old method of cooking hand-made tortillas is still the same. The tortilla is placed on the hot comal. The tortilla cooks on the comal a few minutes until one side is done, then is turned over to finish cooking. It is turned over only one more time·to prevent it from getting tough. There is a saying in Mexico that if the tortilla puffs up, the young girl cooking it will get married. As each tortilla is done, it is lifted from the comal and kept hot wrapped in a cloth in a small basket. The tortillas are piled one on top of another until all are cooked. Piled in this fashion, the heat is maintained.

Tortillas—Commercial: Nowadays there are modern machines to make the tortillas. These are run by two or more operators. One operator puts the masa into a cylinder that feeds the dough out as a thin layer onto a conveyer belt that transports it to a mechanical cutter to cut the tortillas. Another operator picks up the unused portions of the masa and returns it to the cylinder just before the tortillas are taken by the conveyor belt to a flame below for them to be cooked. An operator waits at the end of the machine to pick the cooked tortillas up and pile them for sale to a line of clients that is sure to be there.

Tortillas in central and southern Mexico are traditionally made of corn dough. However, tortilla recipes from northern Mexico emphasize flour. It is believed that this is because some of the Spaniards who settled in the north preferred their wheat to the new corn. Wheat tortillas contain fat, unlike corn tortillas. Wheat tortillas are rolled rather than flattened in a tortilla press.

In communities where there is a large Latin American population you will probably find tortillas at the grocery store. However, you will prefer the homemade tortillas.

BASIC RECIPES FOR TORTILLAS

TORTILLAS DE MAÍZ
(Corn Tortillas)

If there is a tortilla factory near you, buy the masa. You can use your hands or use an electric mixer to save time mixing the dough. For either method, keep a cup of water handy for dipping hands while making tortillas.

1¼ lb. masa   **1 tortilla press**
4 tbsp. water

Preheat griddle until very hot, 475 degrees F to 500 degrees F or 246 degrees C to 260 degrees C.

In a heavy-duty mixer on stir speed, mix masa with the 4 tablespoons water. Add more water if dough continues to be dry, 4 tablespoons at a time.

Shape dough into 12 1-inch balls. Place 2 sheets of cellophane on tortilla press, place a ball of dough on the center of the tortilla press, and shut. Carefully remove cellophane from tortilla. Bake on hot griddle for 30 seconds and turn. Cook 1 minute more and turn; then cook 15 to 30 seconds more. Transfer cooked tortillas to basket lined with cloth napkin so they will keep warm. Makes 12 6-inch tortillas.

Masa Harina Corn Tortillas

If you are unable to purchase fresh masa, Quaker makes a good corn flour called Masa Harina and it is delicious. Cornmeal is not a substitute.

2 cups Corn Masa Harina   **1 tsp. salt**
1⅓ cups lukewarm water

Mix dough and make tortillas as in the above basic recipe. Makes 12 6-inch tortillas.

TORTILLAS DE HARINA O DE TRIGO
(Flour or Wheat Tortillas)

These tortillas are very popular in northern Mexico.

3 cups unsifted all-purpose flour
   (or wheat)
½ tsp. baking powder
½ tsp. salt

½ cup vegetable shortening
1 cup warm water
Oil

In a heavy-duty mixer on stir speed, mix flour, baking powder, salt, and vegetable shortening until it resembles coarse grain, about 2 minutes. Mix in water and beat 1 minute more. Turn dough out onto a smooth surface; knead about 3 minutes. Coat dough with a little oil and put into a plastic bag. Let stand at room temperature for about 1 hour.

Preheat griddle to 425 degrees F (218 degrees C).

Shape into 12 balls. With a rolling pin, flatten each ball into a 6-inch circle. Bake on hot griddle until lightly browned for 30 seconds and turn. Cook 1 minute more and turn; then cook 15 to 30 seconds more. Transfer cooked tortillas to basket lined with cloth napkin so they will keep warm. Makes 12 tortillas.

Instant Flour Tortilla Mix: There are several popular brands of instant flour tortilla mixes available which you can purchase at your grocery store.

CHAPTER 2
BEANS

Beans generally constitute a very important staple in the Latin American daily diet. The importance of beans is not restricted to Mexico, Central America, and the Caribbean Islands. The South American continent has a wide assortment of beans. In Venezuela, the black bean is well liked and is called *caraota*. In Chile, the white bean is known as *poroto* and is used in many recipes.

''Add more water to the beans'' is the famous phrase used when unexpected guests arrive at the dinner hour. There is always room for one more caller at a Mexican table.

Beans are an essential protein source. They contain little fat. They are rich in amino acids, and when eaten in combination with other grains yield a protein nearly as complete as that of animal origin. The ''modest bean'' is rich in Vitamin B, iron, carbohydrates, phosphorous, and traces of other nutrients.

Among the many varieties of beans in Mexico the most popular are the following:

Black Beans (Nickname ''Veracruzanos''): almost ¼ inch long, black with white mark on side (a favorite bean in southern Mexico, especially the state of Morelos)

Canario Beans: yellowish, ⅓ inch long (a favorite bean in central and southern Mexico), hard to find outside of Mexico

Bayo Beans: pink, almost ⅓ inch long (a favorite bean in central and southern Mexico)

Pinto Beans: light pink, mottled with brown, ⅓ inch long (favorite bean in northern Mexico)

Kidney Beans: ½ inch long, reddish brown, imported from Canada to Mexico when there is a shortage of any other kind of beans

In the "olden days" up until the late fifties, most Mexican kitchens could be found simmering an earthenware pot of beans for one to two hours in the morning. These beans had swelled overnight in a pot covered with water to shorten cooking time. The cook would stir them every now and then with a wooden spoon to check their consistency. During the last thirty minutes, salt and sprigs of *epazote* were added to the beans. These beans had a unique flavor acquired from the clay pot they cooked in. Earthenware pots are still the mainstay of humbler Mexican kitchens.

BASIC RECIPES FOR BEANS

FRIJOLES DE OLLA MODERNA
(Modern Beans in a Pot)

The modern Mexican homemaker who lives in the city rejects the slow and laborious earthenware pot and insists on a pressure cooker or metal pot for cooking beans. But the wooden spoon still remains in use.

2 cups dry beans
Water to cover
2 cloves garlic, whole

1 tsp. chicken bouillon
Salt to taste

Remove any foreign matter from beans; rinse in a colander under running water. Put the beans in a large pot, cover with water, and place on high heat. Add garlic. Let boil 10 minutes; reduce heat and semi-cover; let simmer for 1½ to 2 hours (depending on size of beans). Add some boiling water to the beans if they get dry; semi-cover again.

During the last 30 minutes of cooking beans discard the garlic, add the chicken bouillon and salt. Stir and let simmer last 30 minutes or until beans are tender. Serves 6.

Variation: Frequently, when cooking beans, the Mexicans like to add chopped onion, chopped tomato, and whole serrano chilies.

FRIJOLES REFRITOS
(Refried Beans)

Refried beans are very important to Mexican cooking. They are served as a side dish, to decorate another dish, to fill tortillas, and even on French bread—be sure to try the *mollete* recipe in the Breakfast chapter (see index).

6 cups cooked beans
½ cup corn oil
3 corn tortillas

1 cup favorite white cheese, grated
1 bunch radishes, cut in florets

In a mixing bowl, mash the beans with a potato masher. In a heavy frying pan with ¼ cup hot oil, pour the mashed beans. Mash with a large spoon until the beans condense—it takes about 15-20 minutes.

With a sharp knife, slice the tortillas into triangles and fry the tortilla wedges in a heavy frying pan with ¼ cup oil until crispy. Drain on paper towels. These are called *totopos*.

Serve the beans garnished with 2-3 totopos standing in the beans. Sprinkle with favorite white grated cheese and decorate with radishes cut in florets. Serves 6.

Variation: Add to the refried beans 1 cup Manchego or Jack cheese and chilies (sliced in rounds) 5 minutes before beans condense. In Mexico this variation is referred to as *frijoles maneados*.

Main Dish Variation: Preheat oven to 350 degrees F (176 degrees C). Grease an oven-proof ring-shaped mold (with a hollow tube in the center) and fill with refried beans. Spread some butter over the beans and bake for 20-25 minutes or until the beans brown. Invert the mold onto an oven-proof serving platter. Fill center of mold with one of the following of your preference: scrambled eggs or shredded beef or pork. Lower oven heat to warm; transfer platter to oven until ready to serve. Garnish with grated Manchego or Jack cheese, onion rings, sliced radishes, and totopos.

CARNE ENFRIJOLADA
(Beans with Meat)

There is nothing better than coming home on a cold day to find Luis has been simmering these beans for everyone.

3 cups dry beans	**2 tomatoes**
Water to cover	**6 serrano chilies, whole**
2 cloves garlic, whole	**1 tsp. granulated beef bouillon**
1 lb. pork or beef, in 1-inch cubes	**Salt to taste**
3 Mexican chorizos or smoked pork	
sausage	

In a large pot, cover beans with water, bring to a boil, add garlic, and let boil 10 minutes. Add in pork, reduce heat, and let simmer semi-covered for 1½ to 2 hours.

In a heavy frying pan, fry the chorizo over medium heat until crispy. Drain on paper towels, and when cool crumble. Chop tomatoes. Remove stems from chilies.

During the last 30 minutes of cooking beans, discard whole cloves of garlic. Mix in bouillon, crumbled chorizo, chopped tomatoes, and whole chilies. Adjust salt. Serves 6.

CHAPTER 3
CHILIES

Approximately 470 years ago, a Spaniard from Extremadura named Hernan Cortez, later known as the "Conquistador of Mexico," headed three caravels towards Mexico in search of gold and fame. They stopped in Cuba to replenish their supplies and to rest. As soon as Cortez and his men were up to it, they sailed and arrived at what is now known as the port of Veracruz, Mexico. Upon landing, Cortez had his men burn the wooden vessels they had traveled in. This ensured that his men would not return to their native Spain. Cortez conquered the Aztec Empire and the surrounding areas with the help of these men who had no choice but to assist him, and with the further aid of more than 10,000 Tlaxcaltecas who opposed the Aztecs. The Grand Tenochtitlan (now Mexico City) and Emperor Montezuma were doomed.

Cortez' men had left Europe at a time when spices were associated with the elite. Spices had to be shipped to Europe from the Far East and the Middle Eastern countries and were expensive. The Spaniards in the New World were used to and missed this indulgence. They longed for their native *Crocus sativus* (saffron) used to make their *arroz con pollo,* a dish that cannot be made without it.

The Aztecs cherished their local spices and, among them, they had an unlimited variety of chili pods (*Capsicum annum*—the species domesticated in Mexico). They came in all sizes and shapes, some green, some red, some yellow, and some brown. The Spaniards admired the New World food spiced with chilies. The indigenous people bit into the hottest chili as if it were a radish. Some of the recipes called for doses of chilies that would knock the average foreigner off his feet. The Spaniards generally became desensitized to capsaicin, the irritating chemical abundant in chilies.

Growing Chilies: All you have to do to plant your own crop of chilies is to throw seeds from any chilies (dry or fresh) on the dirt. Birds have been doing this for centuries. The only drawback to getting back what you planted is that sometimes the chilies cross-pollinate and just when you expect a hot variety you find that it has crossed with a mild variety.

Popular Chilies: The most popular chilies in Mexico are (1) serrano; (2) Jalapeño; and (3) Poblano, which is preferred for stuffing and making chili strips called *rajas*. The first two are generally easy to find outside of Mexico. The poblano chili is seasonal (August). If the poblano chili is unavailable, substitute the Anaheim or California chili—the mellow bell pepper is not a permissible substitute for the poblano.

CHARACTERISTICS OF VARIOUS CHILIES

Anaheim: light green, long (4 inches), narrow; mild to hot; used both fresh and dried

Ancho: light reddish-brown, mild to hot, dried poblano

de Arbol: rich green, slightly hot, 2½ inches long, most often used dried

de California: also known as Anaheim chili (see above)

Cascabel: dark red, small (1 inch in diameter), round, very hot; dried Manzano chili (*cascabel* means rattle—like the jingles the jesters wore on their outfits while performing for royalty)

Chilaca: identical to Anaheim chili

Chipotle: deep rust-brown; dried, pickled, and/or preferably smoked Jalapeño so that it has its own sauce; extremely hot

Jalapeño: dark green, short (1-3 inches), used fresh and pickled, varying hotness

Japonés: light red, dried serrano chili

Manzano: Apple-shaped, pale yellow, 1 inch in diameter, usually used dried—see *cascabel*

Mulato: dark reddish-brown, mild to hot, dried poblano

Pasilla: dark-brown, mild, dried Chilaca chili

Pequín: dull red, small and tapering (⅜-inches long); used fresh, pickled, or dried and ground to sprinkle over corn on the cob, fresh jicama, or pozole

Poblano: dark green, long and broad (4 x 3 inches), similar to the Anaheim; mild to hot; used both fresh and dried; the preferred chili for making stuffed chilies poblano and rajas; a seasonal chili—appearing around September for three months each year

Serrano: dark green, short and narrow (1½ x 2 inches), usually very hot, when dried called *japonés*

TIPS ABOUT CHILIES

Contact with Chilies: If capsaicin gets into your eyes or any sensitive area, it will sting. Use rubber gloves if you are not yet desensitized to working with chilies. Capsaicin is soluble in alcohol. Washing your hands in rubbing alcohol will soothe the stinging sensation. The pain lasts for a scheduled five minutes. Capsaicin will not wash off painful areas with water or soap. The flaming pain in the mouth will not be lessened by sugar, bread, or cold refreshment. Only time will cure the pain.

Preparing Fresh Poblano Chilies: Chilies must be peeled, deveined, and seeded in preparation for filling them or making strips of them. It is a simple process that can be accomplished on a comal or a griddle. Heat the comal to medium heat and add the chilies (or if you have a gas stove place chilies on low flame), turning until all the sides have black roasted spots on them. The idea is to roast the skin without damaging the chili itself. Place the roasted chilies in a paper or cellophane bag to sweat for 5 minutes. Remove chilies one by one, closing bag so steam does not escape, and remove skin. Let a trickle of water run over chili to remove excess pieces of skin. Make one slit down the side and remove all or some of the seeds inside. This is where you control the heat of the recipe. That is all there is to it.

Preparing Dried Chilies (Pasillas, Anchos, Mulatos): Wash the chilies in cool water to remove dusty particles. Dry chilies with paper towel. Roast the chilies on a hot griddle, turning frequently to roast all sides. The chilies will puff slightly. Do not burn them. Remove the stems, slit the chilies lengthwise, and remove the seeds and veins. Soak the roasted chilies in a small pan of room-temperature water; let stand 15-20 minutes. Reserve the water for later use in thinning or flavoring of the sauce.

CHILES ENCURTIDOS TRADICIONALES
(Traditional Pickled Chilies)

These chilies may cause your eyes to water because they release their sting when they boil. Better get your goggles out.

1 lb. jalapeño or serrano chilies	1 tsp. thyme
1 large white onion	3 tsp. salt
2 carrots	3 tsp. whole black pepper
4 cloves garlic, whole	1 cup vinegar (preferably red wine)
2 bay leaves	Water to cover
1 tsp. oregano	2 10-inch standard canning jars

On a cutting board, slice chilies in strips or halves on the diagonal. Slice the onion on the diagonal and the carrots in rounds. Peel garlic. Transfer the first four ingredients to a heavy pot with the spices, cover with the vinegar and enough water to immerse all the ingredients in liquid. Cover pot, bring to a boil, reduce heat, and simmer 10 minutes. Let come to room temperature. Transfer to canning jars and close lids. There is no need to refrigerate until after you open the jars. Fills 2 10-inch jars.

CHILES TENTADORES EN VINAGRE
(Tempting Pickled Chilies)

The first time you taste these chilies you will become a devotee of this recipe. The credit goes to Luis for creating this original version. Unlike the traditional method of first boiling the chilies and carrots and then pickling them, this method simply pickles them raw. They are so delicious, and it takes so much time for them to season, that anyone in your house might take one before they are ready. Hide them so the jar will not be empty by the time they are ready.

1 lb. serrano chilies	3 tsp. salt
½ lb. pearl (Cambray) onions	3 tsp. whole black pepper
¼ lb. carrots	Red wine vinegar to cover
2 cloves garlic, whole	2 tbsp. corn oil
2 bay leaves	2 10-inch standard canning jars
¼ tsp. oregano	

On a cutting board, slice chilies in halves on the diagonal. Cut pearl onions in half. Slice the carrots in rounds. Peel garlic. Transfer the first four ingredients to jars with spices and cover with vinegar and corn oil, leaving a 1-inch space at top of jars. The oil serves as a sealant. No wax is necessary. Close lid tightly. Let stand one month at room temperature for best results. Good luck keeping those chile lovers out of the jars. Fills 2 10-inch jars.

PART II
MEXICAN CUISINE

Roasted or cooked, corn remains the food par excellence of the Mexicans.
Photography courtesy of Lic. Enrique Figueroa, director of public relations,
Industrias Vinícolas Pedro Domecq, S.A. de C.V.

Marcelina Peña Vda. de Juarez. Photography courtesy of H. V. Lemley, president, Tlapaneco Mission, Inc.

A Tlapaneco indigenous woman making tortillas in Tlacoapa, state of Guerrero, Mexico. Photography courtesy of Rubén Gaytan.

Beans in an earthenware pot. Photography courtesy of Rubén Gaytan.

Fresh sauce (salsa fresca). Photography courtesy of Rubén Gaytan.

Guacamole. Photography courtesy of Rubén Gaytan.

Ground beef empanadas. Photography by Luis Peinado.

Tostadas. Photography courtesy of María Orsini.

Shredded beef (salpicon). Photography courtesy of Rubén Gaytan.

Shrimp soup. In the soup are little tortilla balls. Photography courtesy of María Orsini, editor of *María Orsini: El Arte del Buen Comer (María Orsini: The Art of Eating Well)*.

Chicken with mole. Photography courtesy of María Orsini.

Meatballs in Chipotle Chili Sauce (albóndigas). Photography by Luis Peinado.

Rajas with onion and chicken. Photography courtesy of Rubén Gaytan.

Fresh corn euchepos. Photography by Luis Peinado.

Mexican sweet breads. Photography courtesy of
María Orsini.

Little ears (orejitas). Photography courtesy of
María Orsini.

A basket of bolillos and conchas with pincers. Photography courtesy of
Rubén Gaytan.

Buñuelos and limes filled with coconut. Photography courtesy of María
Orsini.

Flan. Photography courtesy of María Orsini.

Rice pudding (arroz con leche). Photography courtesy of María Orsini.

Pistachio cake. Photography by Luis Peinado.

Mexican sweets with some ingredients. Photography courtesy of María Orsini.

A Mexican candy shop. Citron and pumpkin candies are in the foreground.
Photography courtesy of María Orsini.

CHAPTER 4
BASIC MEXICAN HOT SAUCES

As late as the 1950s, traditional Mexican kitchens were laborious workplaces where numerous servants were needed to prepare time-consuming dishes. For grinding and blending ingredients they used a technique that descended from Aztec times, employing a pestle referred to as a *tejolote* and a *molcajete,* a three-legged mortar usually made of pocked volcanic stone. The work was tedious, but servants were cheap and plentiful. Each household could afford to employ a woman cook and the results were rewarded with plentiful and delicious meals. Molcajetes are still the mainstay of humbler Mexican kitchens and are still on sale in stores and marketplaces. Today the Mexican homemaker who lives in the city disdains the slow and laborious molcajete and demands a blender to grind ingredients.

The blender saves time, but the flavor is not the same. The way to differentiate a salsa made in the blender from a salsa made in the molcajete is this: the blender creates foam. The molcajete would never cause foam that persists for a long time. The only way to get rid of the foam is to cook the salsa, as in *salsa ranchera*.

If you are going to purchase a molcajete, we recommend that you purchase the black basalt molcajete. Inferior molcajetes are a dark grayish color or, even worse, light gray. The inferior grayish-colored molcajetes will release bits of volcanic stone into the salsa.

The salsas served outside of Mexico, though savory, are generally a pseudoversion. The salsas that follow reflect the Mexican repertoire. In them you will find traditional flavors and ingredients presented in ways that emphasize the substance of authentic Mexican salsas.

Preparation of Salsa in Molcajete: This recipe is provided so you will know how to use your black basalt molcajete like an actual Mexican cook. It can be used instead of a blender with any of the following salsa recipes, including guacamole.

(1) Garlic and salt are ground with a stone pestle in a black basalt molcajete (the three-legged mortar);

(2) Chili is then added and ground with the stone pestle;

(3) Tomatoes (or tomatillos—and perhaps cilantro) are added and ground with the stone pestle;

(4) Sections of avocado are added last (if you are making guacamole) and slightly crushed with stone pestle. Do not mash; leave some pieces whole.

BASIC SALSA RECIPES

SALSA FRESCA
(Mexican Fresh Sauce)

This is one of the most popular Mexican salsas. Some people call it "fresh sauce." In northern Mexico they call this salsa "chicken's beak." It is necessary to finish this sauce the same day it is served because of the onion and cilantro. We omit the onion and the cilantro when we know there will be leftovers that have to be refrigerated.

Water
3 tomatoes
4 to 6 serrano chilies
½ white onion

¼ cup fresh cilantro (also known as coriander)
2 tsp. lime juice
Salt to taste

In a small pan bring water to a boil. Briefly immerse tomatoes in boiling water. With a slotted spoon, remove tomatoes, and when cool peel the tomato skins.

In a blender, chop the chilies, onion, and rinsed cilantro leaves (do not use cilantro stems). Transfer this chopped chili mixture to a mixing bowl. With two sharp knives, chop the tomatoes into fine dice and mix with the chili mixture. Add lime juice and salt and let stand for an hour. Serve this sauce in an earthenware sauce dish. Serves 4 to 6.

GUACAMOLE

The avocado, indigenous to Mexico and Guatemala, was introduced to much of South America in pre-Columbian days. Outside of Latin America, commercial avocado production is limited to two areas: southern California and southern Florida. The avocado requires a mild climate to thrive. For guacamole, we recommend the Haas, which is a dark-skinned fruit of medium size. The flesh is rich and buttery with superb flavor. Haas is in season from April through October. Do not mash your avocado: chop it with two sharp knives for better flavor and presentation.

1 recipe Mexican Fresh Sauce   **3 large ripe avocados**
 (see previous recipe)

Prepare Mexican Fresh Sauce and just before serving add the avocados to this tomato sauce by chopping the avocados with two sharp knives.

Serve in an earthenware dish—place an avocado pit in the dish and cover with the guacamole. The avocado pit keeps the sauce from discoloring. Guacamole is served as a salsa, a garnish, or a sauce in which to dip tortilla chips. Serves 4 to 6.

SALSA RANCHERA
(Ranch Sauce)

3 large tomatoes, peeled   **¼ cup water**
4 to 6 serrano chilies   **3 tbsp. corn oil**
½ medium onion   **Salt to taste**

In a blender, briefly blend tomatoes, chilies, and onion with the water. Turn blender on and off about three times; be careful not to overblend. Heat oil in heavy frying pan, add tomato sauce, and simmer for 2-3 minutes. Adjust salt. Serves 4 to 6.

Roasted Version of Ranch Sauce: Place a sheet of aluminum foil on a griddle, turn heat to medium, and let griddle get hot. Roast the whole tomatoes, chilies, and onion on hot griddle until they blister. Do not burn. In a blender, grind the roasted ingredients with the water as in the basic recipe.

SALSA VERDE
(Green Tomatillo Sauce)

When you select your tomatillos, pull the husks back slightly to check the color. If you see that the tomatillos are yellow and swollen, they might be too ripe; if they are dark green and hard they are not yet ripe. They should be light green and firm.

15 green tomatillos
4 to 6 serrano chilies
½ onion
¼ cup water

2 tbsp. cilantro leaves
3 tbsp. corn oil
Salt to taste

Remove husks from tomatillos. Rinse under cool running water. Place a 5-quart pot ½ full of water on stove and bring to boil. Add rinsed tomatillos to pot of boiling water, reduce heat to medium, and let tomatillos simmer for 5-10 minutes, until just tender. Remove tomatillos from hot water with slotted spoon.

In blender, grind tomatillos, chilies, and onion with ¼ cup water, being careful not to overblend. Turn blender off. Add the rinsed cilantro leaves (do not use cilantro stems), and turn blender on and off three times.

Heat oil in heavy frying pan, add tomatillo sauce, and simmer for 5-8 minutes. Adjust salt. Serves 4 to 6.

Roasted Version of Tomatillo Sauce: Remove husks from tomatillos; rinse tomatillos under cool running water. Dry tomatillos with a paper towel. Roast the whole tomatillos, chilies, and onion on hot griddle over medium heat until they blister and brown slightly, 8-9 minutes. Do not burn. Grind roasted ingredients in blender and follow rest of basic recipe.

SALSA PASILLA
(Pasilla Sauce)

Pasilla sauce is served with tortilla dishes and egg dishes. The flavor is unique and one that is acquired. For those who lived in Mexico and forgot to get the recipe, here it is.

3 pasilla chilies
¼ cup warm water
2 tomatoes
3 serrano chilies
½ onion

1 clove garlic
1 tsp. vinegar
Salt to taste
3 tbsp. corn oil

Rinse pasilla chilies, removing any dust particles. Dry chilies with a paper towel. On a hot griddle over medium heat, roast the pasilla chilies. They will puff a little. When roasted on all sides (about 1-2 minutes on each side), remove from griddle and let cool. Remove stems, slice down sides, and remove seeds and veins. Let pasilla chilies rest in the warm water for 20 minutes. Then on the same hot griddle roast the tomatoes, serrano chilies, onion, and garlic (about 5-8 minutes). In a blender, grind the pasilla (with the water), tomatoes, serrano chilies, onion, garlic, and vinegar. Adjust salt to taste. In a heavy sauce pan heat oil and simmer pasilla sauce for about 5 minutes. Keep at room temperature until ready to use. Serves 4 to 6.

SALSA DE CASCABEL
(Cascabel Sauce)

The round, dark red and very hot dry cascabel chili is seldom found in supermarkets or Latin grocery stores in the United States, but its flavor is unique, so if you ever visit Mexico bring some back or have a friend down there send you some.

2 to 3 cascabel chilies
¼ cup warm water
2 tomatoes
¼ onion

2 cloves garlic
2 tbsp. corn oil
Salt to taste

Rinse the chilies under cool running water to remove dust particles. Dry with paper towel. On a hot griddle, roast the chilies about 1-2 minutes; they will puff a little. Let cool. Remove stems but do not discard seeds. Transfer roasted chilies to bowl with the warm water and let sit 20 minutes.

Roast tomatoes, onion, and garlic on hot griddle over medium heat until they blister and brown slightly, 8-9 minutes. Blend roasted ingredients in blender with chilies (and their water). Heat oil in heavy frying pan and sauté for 5-6 minutes. Adjust salt. Serves 4 to 6.

CHAPTER 5
BREAKFAST

Whatever their social status, Mexicans long for their hot dark coffee as soon as they wake up. The breakfast habits of big city dwellers vary from the small town people and peasants in the countryside.

Most of the professional bureaucrats or students who live in Mexico City are used to having their breakfast in an eatery on their way to work or school. If you happen to be in one of the hundreds of eateries or restaurants around 7:00 or 8:00 A.M. you will see that they are crowded and the waiters or waitresses are carrying the famous *huevos rancheros, huevos a la mexicana,* or *molletes*.

Housewives from the province have the custom of rising one or two hours before the rest of the family to cook the beans and prepare or buy the tortillas that will go with chilies or hot sauce. The smell of the cooking beans permeates the house by the time everyone rises for their coffee or their less expensive atole.

But let's not forget that the American influence has given to Mexican children corn flakes or oatmeal for breakfast and on weekends they now like to have pancakes with butter and syrup.

HUEVOS RANCHEROS
(Ranch-Style Eggs)

On each individual plate serve two fried tortillas with one fried egg on top of each tortilla. Top this with three tablespoons of ranch sauce and to one side serve refried beans and a slice of your favorite white cheese. Accompany with buttered toast served on individual bread plates.

1 recipe ranch sauce (see index)	**12 corn tortillas**
1 recipe refried beans (see index)	**12 large eggs, fried**
¼ cup corn oil	**12 slices buttered toast**

You first need to make your salsa. Then, if you are going to serve refried beans, you need to prepare the beans.

Heat oven to 150 degrees F (65 degrees C). Heat oil in heavy frying pan and when hot fry tortillas until pliable. Drain on paper towels and place 2 tortillas on individual oven-proof plates. Place plates with tortillas in warm oven.

The easiest way to fry eggs is to sprinkle the eggs with a little water and steam them, covered. This will prevent the egg yolks from breaking and the edges from browning.

Place one fried egg on each fried tortilla and return to warm oven until process is complete. When ready to serve cover the eggs with sauce. Place beans and cheese slice on side of each plate; serve toast on separate bread plates. Serves 6.

Variation: Make the green tomatillo sauce (see index) instead of the ranch sauce.

TORTILLA ESPAÑOLA DE HUEVO
(Spanish Egg Omelet)

An exception to the rule of "cooking an egg slowly" is the Spanish omelet, when the eggs must be cooked over high heat. This delicious Spanish dish has become popular in Mexico for a light snack or supper.

2 large red potatoes	**1 cup smoked ham, minced**
¾ cup corn oil	**Salt and pepper to taste**
5 large eggs	

Peel potatoes and slice in thin rounds. Heat ¼ cup oil in 10-inch heavy frying pan and fry potatoes until fully cooked, but not browned. Drain on paper towels.

In a 5-quart mixing bowl, gently beat eggs with a fork. Add cooked potatoes and ham to these beaten eggs and let sit at room temperature for 10-15 minutes.

Heat ½ cup oil in 10-inch skillet until it is very hot (otherwise the eggs will stick). Transfer eggs to the frying pan, tilt slightly so eggs will cover bottom of frying pan, and lower heat to medium-high. Shake the pan occasionally to prevent sticking. Once the eggs begin to brown underneath flip the omelet onto a platter of a larger size, add more oil to the skillet, and slide the omelet back into the skillet to brown on the other side. Lower the heat and flip the omelet three times to brown well on both sides. It will remain juicy inside. Add salt and pepper to taste. Serve sliced in pie wedges. Accompany with ranch sauce (see index). Serves 3.

HUEVOS COCIDOS AL HORNO
(Baked Eggs with Sauce)

2 large tomatoes
½ white onion
2 chipotle chilies (smoked, in a can)
¼ cup corn oil

½ stick corn oil margarine
6 oven-proof earthenware
  (individual) dishes
12 eggs
12 slices buttered toast

There is no need to peel tomatoes, just slice tomatoes and onion in quarters and placc in blender with chipotle chilies (add some smoked sauce from the can).

Heat oil in heavy saucepan; sauté this sauce for 4-5 minutes.

Preheat oven to 350 degrees F (176 degrees C). Place a slice of margarine in each individual earthenware dish. Transfer the 6 individual dishes to a cookie sheet. Place the cookie sheet with individual dishes in hot oven for margarine to melt (about 3 minutes).

Remove cookie sheet from oven and break 2 eggs in each dish with melted margarine. Over the raw whole eggs pour 5-6 tablespoons sauce. Once the process is complete, return them to oven. Let bake for 10-15 minutes (or until eggs are cooked).

Accompany with buttered toast. Serves 6.

HUEVOS CON CHORIZO
(Eggs with Mexican Chorizo Sausage)

Due to the great variety of Mexican chorizo sausage this egg dish is very popular.

1 tbsp. oil   10 large eggs, scrambled
12 oz. (or 1½ cups) Mexican chorizo
  sausage
  (see recipe below)

Heat oil in a heavy 10-inch frying pan over medium heat. Remove chorizo from casing and crumble into hot frying pan. The chorizo will release grease; keep moving it with a fork gently until the grease is released and the chorizo's meat is reddish brown. Drain the excess grease from the frying pan, add the eggs, and scramble gently with a fork until the eggs set.

Accompany with fresh corn tortillas (see index) and Modern Beans in a Pot (see index). Serves 6.

CHORIZO MEXICANO
(Mexican Chorizo Sausage)

¼ cup pasilla chili, ground (without   ½ tsp. sugar
  seeds)   ½ cup boiling water
¼ cup ancho chili, ground (without   1 tsp. salt
  seeds)   ½ lb. ground beef
¼ tsp. ground cloves   ½ lb. ground pork
¼ tsp. ground cinnamon   ¼ cup red wine vinegar
2 cloves garlic, minced   ½ cup corn oil
1 tsp. oregano, crushed   Sausage casings

In a small mixing bowl, combine the first eight ingredients, make a paste by adding the boiling water and stirring with a spoon until smooth. In a large mixing bowl on stir speed, mix the ground beef, pork, vinegar, and chili paste until it becomes a red-orange color. Cover and transfer to refrigerator to season 8 hours or overnight.

In a heavy skillet, heat corn oil and sauté mixture until crumbly and partially cooked, stirring often. Let cool. Pack in sausage casings and freeze. Just before using thaw and pan-fry. Serves 6.

MACHACA DE HUEVO
(Dried Shredded Beef with Eggs)

The northern states of Sonora, Chihuahua, Coahuilla, Nuevo Leon, and Durango in Mexico are cattle country and produce a special sun-cured salted beef called *machaca*. This recipe has been adapted to shredded beef because of the difficulty in obtaining the sun-cured salted beef. It can be eaten for breakfast or for a light lunch.

1 tomato
¼ onion
¼ cup corn oil
½ lb. leftover shredded roast beef

8 large eggs, scrambled
Salt to taste
12 flour tortillas

In a mixing bowl, with two sharp knives, chop the tomato and onion.

In heavy frying pan, heat oil over low heat. Fry cooked shredded beef in heated pan. Break eggs into the beef, and scramble with a fork (gently). When eggs set slightly, add the chopped fresh tomato sauce, keep heat on low, and continue simmering for about 3-5 minutes, until eggs set. Adjust salt. When ready to serve heat a comal and warm the flour tortillas. Place in a napkin-lined basket to keep warm. Place basket on table. Accompany with Tempting Pickled Chilies (see index). Serves 6.

HUEVOS A LA MEXICANA
(Mexican-Style Scrambled Eggs)

This dish is as traditional as huevos rancheros in Mexico. Be sure to add the tomato sauce after the scrambled eggs set a little in the frying pan in order to obtain a nice scrambled egg consistency, and also to prevent the eggs from becoming a peculiar color.

¼ onion
4 serrano chilies
2 tomatoes, chopped

¼ cup corn oil
12 large eggs, scrambled
Salt to taste

In a blender chop the onion and chilies. In a mixing bowl, with two sharp knives, chop the unpeeled tomatoes. Add the chili mixture from the blender.

In heavy frying pan, heat oil over low heat. Break eggs into the heated pan, and scramble with a fork (gently). When eggs set slightly, add the chopped fresh tomato sauce, keep heat on low, and continue simmering for about 3-5 minutes, until eggs set. Adjust salt. Accompany with beans in a pot. Serves 6.

MOLLETES

Molletes are good companions to your morning coffee. They are served at Sanborns, Vips, and other coffee shops in Mexico City for breakfast. They are popular among students because they are not only delicious, but also cheap.

6 *bolillos* or French rolls
6 pats butter or margarine
1 recipe refried beans (see index)

1 cup Manchego or Jack cheese, grated
1 recipe ranch sauce (see index)

Preheat oven to 350 degrees F (176 degrees C). Cut the rolls into halves, horizontally. Remove the excess doughy crumbs. Spread 1 pat of butter on the bottom half of each roll. Put halved rolls on cookie sheet and place in oven for 3 minutes, or until crispy. Remove from oven and spread with refried beans and grated cheese. Return to oven another 10 minutes. Serve immediately accompanied with ranch sauce. Serves 6.

CHILAQUILES

In Mexican households chilaquiles are prepared on a weekend morning. Foreigners are generally shy to taste them, but those who take that first bite find them delicious. The best way to make them is to keep the tortillas crispy—not soggy. This recipe is easy to make once you get everything organized. Accompany with refried beans if you like.

12 corn tortillas
¼ cup corn oil
2 to 3 large tomatoes
4 to 6 serrano chilies
½ medium onion
¼ cup water

3 tbsp. corn oil
1 tsp. chicken broth granules
   (Knorr Swiss)
Salt to taste
1 cup Manchego or Jack cheese

With a sharp knife slice the tortillas into 1-inch triangles and fry the tortilla wedges in a heavy frying pan with ¼ cup oil until crispy. Drain on paper towels.

Blend unpeeled tomatoes, chilies, onion and water in blender. Heat 3 tablespoons oil in heavy frying pan, add tomato sauce, and bring to boil. Add chicken granules, adjust salt, reduce heat, and let simmer 4 minutes more.

Grate cheese.

Preheat oven to 350 degrees F (176 degrees C). In an earthenware oven-proof casserole, place the tortilla "chips" (reserve 6 chips for garnishing beans), cover with 2 cups of the sauce, and place in oven for 8-10 minutes. Remove from oven and garnish with grated cheese; return to oven for 2-3 minutes.

Serve immediately accompanied by refried beans with 1 fried tortilla wedge in the beans. Serves 6.

CHAPTER 6
SNACKS

Snacks are sold almost everywhere in Mexico—in *taquerías,* on street corners near government offices, in empty garages near homes, in baskets at the foot of office buildings. It is profitable. Maybe this is why Mexico consumes so many colas.

TACOS DE BISTEC
(Beefsteak Tacos)

½ cup corn oil
4 tbsp. lime juice
1 tsp. pequín chili, ground

Salt and pepper
3 lb. beefsteak
5 bunches pearl onions

In a cruet, mix the corn oil, lime juice, pequín chili, salt, and pepper.

With a meat mallet tenderize the steak so that the marinade will be absorbed. Pour marinade over meat and let stand at least 1 hour (up to 4 hours) in refrigerator.

On a hot grill (or barbecue), grill marinated beef and pearl onions about 6-8 minutes on each side.

Serve with warm corn tortillas (see index) which have been heated on griddle so that each eater can fill his or her own taco and roll it up. Accompany with roasted ranch sauce (see index). Serves 6.

TACOS DE PAPA CON CHORIZO
(Potato and Chorizo Sausage Tacos)

4 large red potatoes
¼ white onion
½ cup corn oil

1 recipe Mexican chorizo sausage
  (see index)
24 fresh corn tortillas (see index)

Peel and cube potatoes; mince onion. Heat ¼ cup oil in heavy frying pan and sauté the potatoes and onion (about 10-15 minutes, until tender, but not browned). Add fried chorizo (which has been drained on a paper towel) to the potato mixture and transfer to a mixing bowl.

Heat tortillas on a griddle. Fill each heated tortilla with chorizo-potato mixture and roll closed. When process is complete, heat ¼ cup oil on medium heat in frying pan. Fry tacos in oil for about 2-3 minutes on each side. Drain tacos on paper towels and serve immediately. Accompany with Mexican Fresh Sauce (see index). Serves 6.

TACOS DE FRIJOLES
(Bean Tacos)

Bean tacos are sold in *taquerías* and fondas, but more often they are sold from a napkin-lined basket—a good idea for a picnic. They are referred to as *tacos sudados* (sweating tacos) because the steam they create keeps them warm.

12 corn tortillas (see index)　　　　**1 recipe refried beans (see index)**

Heat griddle on medium heat and warm tortillas. Fill each warmed tortilla with some refried beans and roll closed. These tacos are not fried.

Accompany with Tempting Pickled Chilies (see index).

SOPES

A *sope* is a small tortilla that has been fried and then garnished. Three are served on an individual dish.

1 recipe refried beans (see index)　　**¼ onion, chopped**
1 recipe ranch sauce (see index)　　　**1 head Romaine lettuce**
5 cups water　　　　　　　　　　　　**1 cup Jack cheese, shredded**
4 chicken breasts　　　　　　　　　　**1 cup plain yogurt**
1 white onion, whole　　　　　　　　　**24 corn tortillas (3½ inches round)**
6 cloves garlic, whole　　　　　　　　　**(see index)**
2 bay leaves　　　　　　　　　　　　　**½ cup corn oil**

Prepare the refried beans and ranch sauce first.

Bring water to boil. Add the chicken breasts, onion, garlic cloves, and bay leaves and let boil 1 minute. Reduce heat to medium, cover, and let chicken simmer for 45 minutes, or until tender. Turn heat off and let chicken cool. Remove chicken from stock and shred chicken. Discard onion, garlic, and bay leaves and reserve the chicken broth for another use.

Slice the ¼ onion in rounds. Rinse the lettuce and cut in 1-inch pieces. Stir the yogurt until softened.

Fry the tortillas in oil until crisp. Drain on paper towels and keep warm in the oven. Spread these toasted tortillas with refried beans and cover with a generous portion of shredded chicken, some ranch sauce, shredded cheese, lettuce pieces, some onion slices, and yogurt. Makes 24 3½-inch *sopes*.

QUESADILLAS

Sold in most fondas and on the streets in Mexico, quesadillas are tortillas stuffed with a favorite filling and fried until the masa is golden.

4 large red potatoes
Water to cover
1 cup mozzarella cheese, shredded

1 cup corn oil
1 recipe masa for corn tortillas (see index)

Peel potatoes and cut in quarters. Place potatoes in a heavy pot and cover with water, bring to a boil, reduce heat, and simmer 15-20 minutes, or until tender.

Remove potatoes from water and mash with potato masher. Mix shredded cheese with mashed potatoes.

Heat oil in a deep frying pan on medium-high heat. Line tortilla press with plastic wrap. Flatten a 1-inch ball of masa in the press. Remove tortilla and fill with some of the potato filling. Fry the quesadilla in the hot oil until golden. Remove with a spatula onto a platter lined with paper towels to drain. Continue process until 12 quesadillas are completed. Serve immediately. Makes 12.

SINCRONIZADAS

Sincronizadas are warm flour tortillas filled with cheese and ham—Mexico's version of the grilled cheese sandwich.

½ lb. Manchego or Jack cheese
12 flour tortillas (see index)

1 lb. ham, thinly sliced

Shred cheese. Warm tortillas on hot griddle, until pliable. Fill each tortilla with some sliced ham and some grated cheese. Return to griddle and warm until cheese melts. Serve immediately accompanied with your favorite salsa. Serves 6.

TORTA DE PUERCO ROSTIZADO
(Roast Pork Torta)

If you talk about a *torta* in South America, you are referring to a cake, but *torta* in Mexico is a Mexican sandwich made of a *telera* or *bolillo* (French bread). The telera is flatter and wider than the bolillo, and filled with a variety of ingredients. The Mexican baked bread is in itself uniquely delicious. *Panaderías* (bakeries) are special places to visit where you can admire the great variety of breads. You would love to eat a freshly baked bolillo still warm from the oven. It is one of the best breads in the world.

Torterias are places where the tortas are sold. They are open all day and some famous torterias in Mexico City are open until midnight.

The most popular tortas are made from roasted pork leg. The recipe set forth below can be varied with any other filling you like. However, the next time you have a pork roast left over try this recipe.

¼ cup corn oil
8 teleras or French rolls
24 thin slices of cold roast pork
2 tbsp. red wine vinegar
¼ tsp. oregano leaves
Salt to taste
2 cups refried beans (see index)

8 slices Manchego or Jack cheese
8 slices tomato
8 slices avocado
8 canned pickled jalapeño chilies in strips
8 tbsp. plain yogurt

Heat oil on a hot griddle. With a sharp knife, cut the telera into halves horizontally. Heat pork slices on hot griddle with vinegar, oregano, and salt. Heat halved teleras on same griddle and then spread the base of the telera with 1 tablespoon of refried beans, 3 slices of roast pork, 1 slice of cheese, 1 slice of tomato, 1 slice of avocado, and 1 or 2 strips of pickled chilies. Add 1 tablespoon of plain yogurt on top of ingredients and cover them with the top of the telera. Makes 8 tortas.

CHAPTER 7
APPETIZERS

In Mexico, appetizers are commonly referred to as *botanas* if accompanied with drinks. Of course, the tendency of the Mexican people to use the diminutive *ita* gives us *botanitas,* and out of this was created a popular verb form *botanear,* which when translated means to munch something while sipping drinks before a meal.

The best botanas to be found anywhere in Mexico are in well-known bars or saloons (*cantinas* in Spanish), which any savvy Mexican male will highly recommend to you. There is such gusto to everything from the simple salty peanuts to the tasty quesadillas, but the prize goes to the picante shrimp broth served in small bowls. Just recently, women have been permitted inside to savor these popular botanas they have heard their menfolk talk about for years.

Below we have selected some botanas you can serve at any dinner or party. Botanas can be made from many combinations and it would be impossible here to make a list of all of them. If some ingredient is not available, substitute another similar ingredient. The cold botanas should be served separate from the warm ones. Botanas are small and delicate and should be served with drinks or fruit juices.

Mexican picante sauces can also serve as botana dips.

WARM APPETIZERS

TAQUITOS DE CARNITAS
(Pork Tacos)

We were tickled to find one guest eating his botana taco with the right hand and holding a napkin over his taco with the left hand. Curious, we asked if everything was okay. He indicated everything was delightful as he lifted his napkin to reveal not one but three taquitos beneath his napkin.

3 lb. pork shoulder
¼ cup corn oil

Salt and pepper to taste
24 3½-inch corn tortillas (see index)

Heat oven to 300 degrees F (148 degrees C). Cut fresh pork shoulder into small, even, 1-inch cubes. Place meat on baking sheet and spread oil on pork. Sprinkle with salt and freshly ground black pepper. Place in heated oven and cook at this temperature for 1½ to 2 hours, or until the pork is crispy.

Heat griddle. Remove pork from oven and heat tortillas on hot griddle. Place 2-3 pieces of pork in each tortilla and roll up into miniature taquitos. Put on a platter, letting each taco press against the other to keep closed. Do not use wooden picks for these appetizers as your guests may inadvertently swallow one. Makes 24 taquitos.

TAQUITOS DE CAMARONES
(Shrimp Taquitos)

1 lb. small shrimp
1 tsp. lime juice
4 cloves garlic
½ white onion
2 jalapeño chilies
1 large tomato
¼ cup corn oil

1 cube fish flavor bouillon
  seasoning (Knorr Swiss)
1 tbsp. Maggi seasoning
Salt to taste
24 3½-inch corn tortillas (see
  index)
¼ cup corn oil

Rinse shrimp under cold running water. Remove shells; with sharp knife remove dark veins. Place cleaned shrimp in bowl with cold water and ice, and lime juice. Place shrimp in refrigerator. After about 10 minutes, drain water and chop shrimp. Mince garlic and chop onion, chilies, and tomato. Heat ¼ cup oil in a heavy frying pan. Brown onion, about 2 minutes. Add garlic and continue browning another 2-3 minutes. Add chilies, then add tomato, bouillon, Maggi, and salt and let simmer another 1 minute.

Add shrimp to sauce mixture and cook until it thickens, about 10 minutes. Remove from stove and place mixture in a bowl.

Heat tortillas on griddle. Fill each tiny tortilla with a teaspoonful of the shrimp filling and roll. Secure the taquitos by pressing each against the other to keep closed —use a large kitchen spoon to keep the first one closed. Do not use a wooden pick to secure, as your guests may inadvertently swallow one. Once they are all rolled with their filling, heat ¼ cup oil in heavy frying pan, and fry the little taquitos until crispy on all sides. Can be kept on ''warm'' (150 degrees F or 65 degrees C) in the oven, but should be served immediately. Makes 24.

EMPANADITAS DE PICADILLO
(Ground Beef Empanadas)

The time spent on making these empanaditas is well rewarded when you see that your guests can't get enough of them. They are guaranteed to disappear off the serving platter first. The beef filling and the pastry must be made "the night before." Few guests will be able to figure out how you kept them so juicy — it's the gelatin.

2 large red potatoes	1 tsp. dry mustard
¼ cup onion	1 tbsp. Worcestershire sauce
½ cup black olives (preferably Calamato)	2 envelopes unflavored gelatin (2 tbsp.)
¼ cup corn oil	½ cup cold water
1 lb. ground meat	1 cup water
1 tsp. pequín or cayenne chili, ground	1 tsp. beef flavor bouillon
½ tsp. cumin, ground	2 eggs
	Salt and pepper to taste

Peel and dice potatoes. Chop onion and olives. Heat oil in a heavy frying pan on high heat and fry ground meat about 5 minutes. Add potatoes and continue frying 5 minutes more. Add ground chili, cumin, dry mustard, minced onion, chopped black olives, and Worcestershire sauce. Cover pan. Lower heat and simmer 25 minutes more, until beef and potatoes are cooked.

In a cup, mix unflavored gelatin with the cold water. In a medium saucepan, bring the 1 cup water to a boil and dissolve beef bouillon in boiling water. Add dissolved gelatin to beef broth and remove from stove. Pour this beef-gelatin broth over the fried ground beef filling and stir. Remove from stove and let come to room temperature. Transfer to a covered mixing bowl and place in refrigerator for 8 hours (overnight). Hard boil eggs, chop, and sprinkle over beef filling just before filling and shaping empanadas. Add salt and pepper to taste.

PASTRY

1 pkg. active dry yeast (¼ oz. or
   7 grams)
1 tbsp. sugar
¼ cup warm water (104 degrees F
   or 40 degrees C)

3½ cups all-purpose flour
1 tsp. salt
½ cup vegetable shortening,
   softened
½ cup + 4 tbsp. warm water

Sprinkle yeast and sugar over ¼ cup warm water in a medium bowl; stir to dissolve. Let stand until foamy, 10-15 minutes.

Sift flour and salt in a mixing bowl.

In a 5-quart bowl, pour the yeast mixture and add softened vegetable shortening. Using a flat attachment on your mixer, mix on stir speed. Add flour mixture, 1 cup at a time, alternately with the water (4 tablespoons at a time). Mix until dough is elastic and forms a ball, about 5 minutes. Do not overbeat or the dough will be tough. Grease large mixing bowl and put in dough. Let dough rise in warm draft-free area until doubled in volume, about 2 hours. Dough should be placed in refrigerator up to 8 hours (overnight) so it will remain a flat dough.

Preheat oven to 400 degrees F (204 degrees C). Grease cookie sheet. Punch dough down and knead on lightly floured surface until elastic, 2 to 3 minutes. Divide dough into ½-inch balls. With rolling pin or tortilla press, flatten dough balls into 4-inch disk shapes.

Remove meat filling from refrigerator. Sprinkle chopped egg on top of filling. With a tablespoon, place 1 tablespoon meat filling in the center of each disk and fold in half.

Tightly seal empanadas so juice will not escape: start from the right side of the arc of each empanada and, using the thumb and the forefinger, pinch the edge and twist. Advance and repeat the operation until you reach the other end of the arc of each empanada. Place each empanada on greased cookie sheet.

When oven is very hot, bake 10-15 minutes at 425 degrees F (218 degrees C) or until dough is golden. Remove from oven on time so the juicy filling will not dry up. Makes 24.

EMPANADAS DE QUESO
(Cheese Empanadas)

The pastry for the cheese empanadas is made with baking powder instead of yeast and filled with grated Manchego or Jack cheese, plus a dash of Tabasco sauce. Prepare the pastry the day before making the empanadas.

3½ cups all-purpose flour
1 tsp. baking powder
1 tsp. salt
½ cup vegetable shortening

½ cup cold water
1½ cups grated Manchego or Jack cheese
1 jar Tabasco sauce

Sift flour, baking powder, and salt in a mixing bowl.

Place shortening in 5-quart mixing bowl. Using a flat beater at stir speed, alternately add in flour and 4 tablespoons cold water until smooth and elastic. Do not overmix as dough will be tough (about 2 minutes). Grease mixing bowl, place dough in it, and refrigerate 8 hours (overnight).

Preheat oven to 400 degrees F (204 degrees C). Grease cookie sheet. Knead dough on lightly floured surface until elastic, 2 to 3 minutes. Divide dough into ½-inch balls. With rolling pin or tortilla press, flatten dough balls into 4-inch disk shapes.

Place 1 tablespoon grated cheese and some Tabasco sauce on each disk. Tightly seal empanadas so melted cheese will not escape: start from the right side of the arc of each empanada and, using the thumb and the forefinger, pinch the edge and twist. Advance and repeat the operation until you reach the other end of the arc of each empanada. Place each empanada on greased cookie sheet.

When oven is very hot, bake 10-15 minutes at 425 degrees F (218 degrees C) or until dough is golden. Remove from oven and serve immediately while cheese is still melted. Makes 24.

ALBONDIGITAS

Few of your guests will figure out that it is the deviled ham that gives these tiny meatballs that special flavor. Not only that, but the deviled ham keeps the tiny meatballs from breaking. Use decorative wooden picks for serving. Be sure to try the regular-size Meatballs in Chili Chipotle Sauce from the Beef chapter (see index) for dinner some day. They also will become your favorite.

3 cloves garlic	1 lb. ground beef
¼ white onion	1 (6 oz.) can deviled ham
4 tbsp. cilantro	4 tbsp. corn oil

In a medium mixing bowl, mince the garlic, chop the onion and cilantro finely, and add the ground beef and deviled ham. Shape into ½-inch balls. Fry the meatballs in oil until they are browned on all sides. Place in warm oven covered with aluminum foil until ready to serve so they will not dry out. Serve with ranch sauce (see index). Serves 6.

QUESO FLAMEADO
(Cheese Fondue)

In good Mexican restaurants they always offer you cheese fondue before you look at the menu.

1 clove garlic, minced	2 tsp. cornstarch
1½ cups white wine	3 tbsp. Tabasco sauce
1 lb. Manchego or Jack cheese, grated	3 tbsp. wine
	6 French rolls, cut in cubes

Rub the bottom and sides of a chafing dish with minced garlic. Add 1½ cups wine and heat almost to a boil, but do not boil.

Add shredded cheese gradually, stirring constantly with a wooden spoon. When the cheese is creamy and almost simmering, add cornstarch blended with Tabasco sauce and wine. Stir until the mixture bubbles.

When cheese is hot transfer to a fondue pot. Serve with French bread, or any favorite crusty bread to be dipped in the cheese fondue. Serves 6 hungry.

CALDO DE CAMARÓN
(Shrimp Broth)

The *hora del amigo* is Mexico's noon "happy hour," and if you happen to be sitting at a bar they will serve you two drinks for the price of one accompanied with a botana. The famous Sanborns eateries generally offer this picante version of shrimp broth when you arrive at the hora del amigo. It is highly recommended that you try this recipe, and the next time you are in Mexico City order some.

If the dry (peeled) shrimp are not available in your area, make this recipe with fresh small shrimp.

½ lb. dry shrimp
1 carrot, peeled
3 cloves garlic
8 cups water
1 tbsp. fish flavor bouillon
   seasoning (Knorr Swiss)

1 small (5 oz.) can tomato puree
1½ tsp. ground pequín chili
Salt to taste

Rinse dry shrimp 10-15 minutes in cold water. (If using fresh shrimp, rinse and devein them.) Dice carrot and mince garlic.

In a large pot, bring 8 cups of water to a boil, add dry shrimp and diced carrot, and reduce heat. Add fish bouillon, minced garlic, tomato puree, and pequín. Cover and simmer for 30 to 45 minutes on low heat or until the dried shrimp are soft. (If using fresh shrimp add shrimp the last 5 minutes.) Adjust salt. Serve in coffee-cup-size bowls. Serves 6.

COLD APPETIZERS

CEVICHE

This popular appetizer is especially delicious. You discard the lime juice just before adding the sauce.

1 lb. fresh red snapper (or substitute any other firm fish)
2 cups lime juice
Salt to taste
1 white onion, chopped
2 large tomatoes, chopped
2 to 4 serrano chilies, chopped

½ tsp. dried oregano
¼ cup cilantro, finely chopped
1 cup catsup
½ cup corn oil
2 tbsp. Worcestershire sauce
1 (7 oz.) jar whole green olives with pimentos

Rinse fish under cold running water. Chop fish in 1- by ½-inch pieces. Place fish pieces in a large glass jar with lime juice. Adjust salt. Cover jar and let fish marinate in refrigerator for 12 hours. The fish will ''cook'' in the lime juice.

Once 12 hours have lapsed, remove fish from refrigerator and drain lime juice completely. Put marinated fish in mixing bowl. Rinse jar thoroughly.

In a separate mixing bowl, place chopped onion, chopped tomatoes, chopped chilies, oregano, cilantro, catsup, corn oil, and Worcestershire sauce. Put sauce in a large covered jar, add fish and olives, and let stand at least 30 minutes. The fish can be kept for 1 day in refrigerator in this sauce.

Serve in seafood cocktail glasses, or on a bed of lettuce garnished with sliced white onion and radishes cut in florets. Serves 6.

COCTEL DE CAMARONES
(Shrimp Cocktail)

Most people boil their shrimp for shrimp cocktail, but you are going to love this sautéed version.

1 lb. medium-sized shrimp	½ cup white wine
Ice water	1 large tomato, chopped
¼ tsp. red wine vinegar	½ cup catsup
2 tsp. corn oil margarine	¼ white onion, chopped
3 cloves garlic, minced	1 serrano chili, chopped
3 tablespoons corn oil	

Peel shrimp all at once, the next process will be to remove vein running down back. Rinse under running water. Put cleaned shrimp in glass bowl with ice water and vinegar (so shrimp will stay fresh).

Drain shrimp on paper towels. Heat margarine with oil in heavy metal frying pan. Add garlic and shrimp and sauté briefly, about 5 minutes on each side. If you overcook, shrimp will become rubbery. When cooked, add wine to frying pan and let simmer 2-3 minutes.

In a blender, mix tomato with catsup, onion, and chili serrano.

Remove shrimp from stove, place shrimp in covered glass mixing bowl, add tomato sauce, and place in refrigerator until ready to serve.

Serve in seafood cocktail glasses or on a bed of lettuce garnished with radishes in florets and green olives.

CHAPTER 8
SOUPS

The Spaniards introduced soup to the Aztec and Maya civilizations and now the Mexicans eat it every day, seven days a week. The Mexicans gave soup their own excellent touch and we have recreated some of these truly Mexican soups for you to savor.

Dinner in Mexican homes is served from 2:00 to 3:00 P.M., and it always starts with a soup. The typical father of a Mexican family will start a quarrel if the soup is not on the table. The soup is followed by "dry soup," which is what they call the rice or pasta part of the meal.

In order to make a memorable soup, you need to have a good stock. Sometimes the pace of life forces us to use canned or granulated stock, but these soups are far inferior in taste and have neither the valuable nutrients obtained from homemade stock nor the lasting memory created by soups made from homemade stock. You will notice that people will always want the recipe of the soup made from your own stock.

CALDO DE POLLO
(Chicken Stock)

6 cups water
3 chicken breasts, with bone and
  skin
1 turnip, whole, peeled

1 bay leaf
2 cloves garlic, whole
1 white onion, whole

In a 5-quart pot bring the water to a boil. Add chicken, whole turnip, bay leaf, garlic, and onion. Let boil for 5 minutes, reduce heat, and let simmer for 45-50 minutes, or until chicken is tender. Remove chicken from stock and set aside for the preparation of other dishes. Discard turnip, bay leaf, garlic, and onion. When stock is cool, with a spoon, skim off fat that forms on top. Serves 6.

CALDO DE RES
(Beef Stock)

6 cups water
1 lb. beef stew meat with soup bone
1 white onion, whole

2 cloves garlic, whole
1 bay leaf, whole

In a large pot bring the water to a boil. Add beef, soup bone, onion, garlic, and bay leaf. Let boil for 5 minutes, reduce heat, and let simmer for 40-45 minutes, or until beef is tender. Remove beef from stock and set aside for the preparation of other dishes. Discard bone, onion, garlic, and bay leaf. When stock is cool, with a spoon, skim off fat that forms on top. Serves 6.

CALDO DE CAMARÓN
(Shrimp Stock)

2 medium tomatoes
4-5 cups water
1 oz. dried shrimp, peeled (whole)

1 white onion, whole
2 cloves garlic, whole

Grind tomatoes in blender. In a 5-quart pot, bring the water to a boil. Add shrimp, onion, garlic, and tomato. Let boil for 5 minutes. Reduce heat and let simmer 40 minutes. Filter stock through a fine sieve to separate shrimp, onion, and garlic from broth. Discard onion and garlic. If dried shrimp are of good quality (like the variety found in Mexico) return shrimp to stock. Otherwise, discard the dried shrimp and just take advantage of the delicious shrimp flavor. Serves 6.

CALDO DE POLLO CON ARROZ
(Chicken with Rice Soup)

This is a common soup in Mexican kitchens. It can be eaten by all members of the family, and its comforting quality makes it the soup of choice to be given to the sick or the children.

1 recipe chicken stock (see index)
1 cup long grain rice

1 cup peas, fresh or frozen (not
    canned)
Salt to taste

In a heavy pan heat chicken stock to boiling. Add rice along with the fresh peas and let cook on low heat for 20 minutes (if using frozen peas add during the last 5 minutes). With a slotted spoon, remove a few grains of rice to see if it is cooked; you may need to cook it 5-10 minutes more, until the rice is tender. Do not overcook the rice because it will break. Adjust salt. Serves 6.

SOPA DE TORTILLA
(Tortilla Soup)

This soup should be called "pick me up" because it will lift your spirits to see the colorful avocado slices and pasilla chilies mixed with the tortilla strips. Mexican housewives are to be thanked for this innovative solution to leftover tortillas.

7 cups water	Salt to taste
2 chicken breasts, with bone and skin	12 corn tortillas
	¼ cup corn oil
2 large tomatoes	3 pasilla chilies
½ medium onion	2 large Haas avocados
1 tsp. Maggi seasoning	1 jar pickled jalapeño chilies

In a heavy soup pot, bring the water to a boil. Add chicken breasts with skin and bone intact. In a blender, grind tomatoes with onion and add to chicken. Season with Maggi. Reduce heat and let chicken simmer 35-40 minutes, until tender. When cool shred chicken and return to soup.

With a sharp knife, slice tortillas into strips. In a heavy frying pan heat the oil on medium heat and fry the tortilla strips until crisp. Drain fried tortillas on paper towels. Heat soup and serve immediately accompanied with these fried tortillas. Serves 6.

Garnishes: In a mixing bowl with warm water, soak the pasilla chilies for 10 minutes just to soften. Dry on paper towels and fry in heavy frying pan 1-2 minutes on each side. Chop pasilla chilies. Slice the avocados in wedges. Transfer them to serving dishes so that each serving will contain some of these. Place jalapeños in bowls to use as a garnish.

CALDO TLALPEÑO
(Tlalpeño Soup)

This soup is on the menu of almost every restaurant because it is simply delicious.

7 cups water	12 sprigs cilantro
3 whole chicken breasts	1 (15 oz.) can garbanzo beans
1 white onion, whole	Salt to taste
3 cloves garlic, whole	2 Haas avocados, sliced
1 bay leaf	1 can chipotle chilies
½ tsp. oregano	3 limes, sliced

In a large pot, bring the water to a boil. Add chicken breasts (halved), whole onion, whole garlic, bay leaf, oregano, and cilantro. Reduce heat to medium and cook for 45-50 minutes. Transfer chicken to platter and shred (discard chicken skin and bones, as well as onion, garlic, bay leaf, and cilantro). Return shredded chicken to clear chicken broth. Drain liquid from garbanzos and pour them into broth; return to stove and let simmer on medium heat for 5 minutes. Serve immediately accompanied with the sliced avocado, chipotle chilies, and the sliced limes in earthenware bowls. Serves 6.

CALDO XOCHITL
(Xochitl's Soup)

This is a "must" soup if you want to try the real Mexican art of preparing soup with some colorful garnish.

5 cups chicken stock (see index)	**2 Haas avocados**
1 serrano chili	**¼ cup cilantro**
3 leeks, peeled	**Salt to taste**
2 large tomatoes	

Prepare chicken stock. Using the 3 chicken breasts from the stock, shred chicken (without bone and skin) and return it to broth.

Use 5 small serving dishes to keep the garnishes separate. Chop chili, leeks, tomatoes, avocados, and cilantro — then place each chopped garnish in its serving dish and then on the table.

Return chicken and broth to stove and bring to boil. Adjust salt. Pour stock with chicken in 6 individual soup bowls. The 5 fresh garnishes will be used to decorate and flavor the soup. Do not stir the garnishes into the soup. The leeks should be sprinkled on last. Serves 6.

SOPA POBLANA DE ELOTE
(Poblano Corn Soup)

This soup is called "Puebla style" because the poblano chili is characteristic of Puebla. If poblano chili is unavailable in your area use California chili; it is somewhat more narrow than the poblano, but it will do the trick.

3 poblano chilies
2 large tomatoes
6 cups chicken stock (see index)
¼ cup corn oil
¼ teaspoon oregano

½ teaspoon pequín chili, ground (optional)
3 cups fresh white corn kernels
Salt to taste

Heat griddle on medium-high. Place a sheet of aluminum foil on it; roast poblano chilies for 5 minutes so the skins will loosen. Transfer to plastic bag to sweat for another 5 minutes. Roast tomatoes on griddle for 3 minutes, turning frequently. In blender grind tomatoes with ¼ cup chicken stock. Remove poblanos, one at a time, from the bag and peel loosened skin, remove stems and seeds, and slice in strips. Heat oil in a large heavy pot and sauté tomatoes on high heat for 3 minutes. Add remaining chicken stock, oregano, pequín (if desired), corn kernels, and poblano strips. Reduce heat to medium and let simmer 3-5 minutes. Adjust salt. Serve immediately. Serves 6.

SOPA DE REPOLLO
(Cabbage Soup)

A hearty soup like this one makes hungry people happy. This soup is so delicious that it will quickly become a family favorite.

8-9 cups water
1 lb. beef stew meat with soup bone
1 medium onion, whole
2 cloves garlic, whole
1 bay leaf, whole
4 carrots, cut in sticks

6 medium red potatoes, halved
2 ears of corn, cut in 12 rounds
1 medium head cabbage
1 large tomato
1 serrano chili, ground
Salt to taste

In a large pot bring the water to a boil. Add beef, soup bone, onion, garlic, and bay leaf. Let boil for 5 minutes, reduce heat, and let simmer for 40-45 minutes. Turn heat off and let cool. When stock is cool and gelled, with a spoon skim off fat that formed on top of stock. Discard the bone, onion, garlic, and bay leaf, saving the beef cubes and stock.

To the beef and stock, add carrots, potatoes, and corn and let simmer for another 30 minutes.

Separate cabbage leaves without cutting them, and add cabbage leaves to soup. Let soup simmer 15 minutes more.

Serve the soup in individual soup bowls and each eater can garnish the soup with the sauce below.

Garnish: Peel tomato and cut in large pieces. Place tomato with serrano chili in blender and grind to a sauce. In a small saucepan heat the sauce over low heat for about 5 minutes, or until sauce has cooked. Adjust salt. Put sauce in a small serving bowl. Serves 6.

SOPA DE CEBOLLA
(Onion Soup)

Traditionally this soup comes from France, but Mexicans have adopted it and they like to order it in restaurants.

2 cups onions, thinly sliced	**Salt and pepper to taste**
4 tablespoons corn oil	**6 slices French bread, each large**
6 to 7 cups beef stock	**enough to span width of bowl**
½ cup white wine	**1 cup Gruyère cheese, grated**

Heat oven to 450 degrees F (232 degrees C).

Heat oil in large heavy pot and fry onions, turning to brown all sides. Lower heat, add beef stock, and simmer for 10 minutes. Add wine, simmer for 2 minutes more, and season with salt and pepper.

Toast the bread until dry; set aside.

Ladle browned onion and beef stock into individual small casseroles. Float the toasted French bread on top of each casserole, followed by a generous sprinkle of cheese. The cheese should extend to the edge of the casserole to help anchor the bread slice. Broil the soup in oven until the cheese melts and begins to bubble. Serve immediately. Serves 6.

Note: Try to be flexible for those members of the family, or friends, who prefer not to have their bread floating in the soup, and offer them the onion soup with their grilled cheese toast on the side of the soup.

SOPA DE AJO
(Garlic Soup)

Traditionally this favorite soup is from the Iberian Peninsula (Portugal and Spain). Due to the many Spaniards making Mexico their home, it is now considered a Mexican soup. You are going to love this one. Traditionally the egg is poached in each individual soup.

1 cup ham	**8 cups beef stock (see index)**
6 cloves garlic	**Salt and pepper to taste**
3 tbsp. corn oil	**6 eggs**

Preheat oven to 400 degrees F (204 degrees C).

Dice ham. With garlic press, mince garlic. In a large heavy pot heat the oil on low heat and sauté ham and garlic for 2-3 minutes. Add beef stock and simmer for 8-10 minutes more; season to taste with salt and pepper.

Place 6 individual oven-proof soup bowls on a cookie sheet and fill ¾ full with boiling stock. Gently break 1 egg into each. Place soup bowls in hot oven so eggs will poach for about 10-15 minutes. Serve immediately. Serves 6.

SOPA DE HONGOS
(Mushroom Soup)

In Mexico there are two classes of people who cook with mushrooms: the farmers who know how to distinguish and pick the safe ones and the very rich people who buy them for their gourmet cooking. They are expensive.

6 cups water	**4 cloves garlic**
1 lb. pork chunks	**3 tbsp. butter or margarine**
2 poblano chilies	**2 large tomatoes**
1 lb. large mushrooms	**Salt to taste**
1 white onion	

In a dutch oven, bring the water to a boil. Add pork chunks and let boil for 1 hour.

On a comal or griddle, toast the poblano chilies for 4 to 5 minutes, place them in a cellophane bag, and let sweat for 10 minutes. Remove chilies from bag and peel skin, remove seeds, and cut in strips.

Clean mushrooms; remove stems. Chop onion. Mince garlic. In a heavy pan over low heat, melt butter, and sauté the mushrooms with the onion and garlic for 5 minutes.

Puree the tomatoes in a blender. Add tomatoes to mushrooms. Continue cooking for 10 minutes.

Add tomatoes and mushrooms to pork and then add poblano chilies. Let simmer for another 20 minutes. Adjust salt. Serves 6.

SOPA DE LENTEJA
(Lentil Soup)

There is no doubt that this soup has been brought from Spain by the Spanish conquistadors. It is so ancient that it is mentioned in the Bible, and there is a saying in all Spanish-speaking countries of the world, ''Never refuse to give lentil soup to a needy one.''

2 cups dry lentils
2 beef wieners, sliced in thin
   rounds
1 ripe plantain, sliced in thin
   rounds
2 fresh carrots, diced

1 tomato, peeled, chopped
¼ small white onion, chopped
2 cloves garlic, minced
¼ tsp. cumin
1 tbsp. red wine vinegar
4 jalapeño chilies, chopped

In a heavy pot, ¾ full with water, place the lentils. Bring to a boil, reduce heat, and let simmer 1 hour.

After the first hour, add the sliced wieners, sliced plantain, diced carrots, chopped tomato, chopped onion, minced garlic, and cumin and continue cooking 30-35 minutes, or until lentils are tender.

Add vinegar the last 5 minutes of cooking. Serve the chopped jalapeños in a side dish for everyone to garnish their soup if desired. Serves 6.

SOPA DE CHÍCHARO SECO
(Split Pea Soup)

Mexico has adopted this Dutch soup as one of its own and so it is included among our favorite Mexican soups.

12 sprigs parsley	2 cloves garlic, minced
2 cups dried green split peas	¼ tsp. cumin
1 meaty ham bone	1 can potato sticks
1 tomato, peeled, chopped	Salt to taste
¼ small white onion, chopped	

Rinse and clean parsley; chop and set aside.

In a heavy pot ¾ full with cool water, place the split peas and bring to a boil. Add ham bone, reduce heat and simmer for 1 hour.

After the first hour, add the chopped tomato, chopped onion, minced garlic, and cumin and continue cooking 30-45 minutes, or until split peas are tender. During the last 5 minutes, add chopped parsley and simmer. Adjust salt. Serve immediately.

Place potato sticks in serving bowl so everyone can garnish their soup if desired. Serves 6.

SOPA DE CAMARONES
(Shrimp Soup)

This has always been a favorite soup, especially during the Lenten season (the forty days of fasting and penitence from Ash Wednesday to Easter) when it is prohibited on Fridays to eat any type of meat other than fish.

36 to 48 medium shrimp	6 small potatoes, quartered
2 ears of corn	1 to 2 jalapeños, whole
2 medium tomatoes	2½ cups milk
¼ cup corn oil	2 egg yolks, beaten
2½ cups shrimp stock (see index)	1½ tbsp. dry sherry
1 bay leaf	Salt to taste

Peel and devein shrimp. Place cleaned shrimp under running water to rinse. Place rinsed shrimp in a mixing bowl full of ice-cold water and a drop of lemon; set aside in refrigerator. Shuck corn, cut each ear into 6 round slices, and set aside. In a small pan with boiling water, briefly immerse tomatoes then peel skins, grind tomatoes in blender, and set aside.

In a heavy soup pot heat oil and sauté tomatoes for 3 minutes. Add shrimp stock and bay leaf and bring to a boil; reduce heat and simmer for 15 minutes. Peel the potatoes. Add the peeled potatoes, sliced corn, and the jalapeños and let simmer for 30 minutes.

Drain the shrimp on a paper towel. Add the shrimp and bring to a boil; reduce heat and simmer for 10 minutes. Add the milk and simmer another 3 minutes. Add egg yolks into soup and stir rapidly. Add sherry, return to heat, cover, and simmer 2 minutes. Adjust salt. Remove jalapeños and bay leaf and serve. Serves 6.

CREAM SOUPS

Cream soups as a rule are special soups served when you are having guests for dinner and there are more dishes to be served. The following cream soups are light and wonderful. They do not include any starchy thickeners because you will see that the vegetable or legume in each recipe thickens the soup when simmered over low heat for fifteen to twenty minutes. We have purposely omitted heavy creams in order to maintain the lightness of each soup.

CREMA DE ALCACHOFAS
(Cream of Artichoke Soup)

Artichokes are common in all Latin American countries and there seems to be no reason for them to be expensive, but in fact they are. The better restaurants in Mexico City offer this cream of artichoke hearts on the menu.

3 (14 oz.) cans artichoke bottoms (or hearts)
4 cups chicken stock
3 tbsp. butter or margarine

3 cups milk
½ tsp. nutmeg
Salt to taste
1 can potato sticks

In a blender, finely grind the artichokes with ½ cup stock. In a large pot heat butter or margarine on medium heat, transfer ground artichokes to heated butter or margarine, and sauté for 2 minutes. Add remaining chicken stock, milk, and nutmeg and let simmer 15 minutes. Adjust salt. Garnish with potato sticks if desired. Serves 6.

CREMA DE FRIJOLES PINTOS
(Savory Cream of Pinto Bean Soup)

It is only natural that beans would not be excluded from the repertoire of Mexican cream soups.

6 corn tortillas
¼ cup corn oil
3 cups cooked pinto beans (see
  Modern Beans in a Pot)

3 cups beef stock (see index)
Salt to taste
1 Haas avocado, sliced
3 serrano chilies, cut in rounds

Slice the tortillas into thin slices. In a deep heavy pot, fry the tortilla pieces in oil until golden. Remove from pot and drain on platter with paper towel.

Grind beans in blender with 1 cup beef stock. Transfer to the large pot, add remaining beef stock, and let simmer 15 minutes, stirring. Season with salt to taste.

Garnish with fried tortilla slices, sliced avocado, and serrano chili rounds. Serves 6.

CREMA DE FRIJOLES NEGROS
(Cream of Black Bean Soup)

Black beans are very popular in the southern part of Mexico and in the Caribbean countries. The eponymous color in a soup might be beyond your imagination, but when we tasted this cream soup while visiting some friends in Chilpanzingo, State of Guerrero, we knew we had to include it in this book.

12 thin bacon slices
3 cups cooked black beans (see
  Modern Beans in a Pot)

5 cups beef stock (see index)
6 eggs

Preheat oven to 375 degrees F (190 degrees C).

In a heavy frying pan, fry the bacon until crispy. Drain on a plate with paper towels; set aside.

Place cooked beans in blender and grind with some beef stock. Transfer beans to large pot, add remaining beef stock, and bring to a boil, stirring. Reduce heat and simmer for 5 minutes, stirring occasionally.

In 6 individual oven-proof soup bowls, fill ¾ full with the bean soup. Break 1 egg in each bowl. Bake in oven until eggs are set, about 10-15 minutes. Garnish with crumbled bacon. Serve immediately. Serves 6.

CREMA DE COLIFLOR
(Cream of Cauliflower Soup)

We highly recommend this easy and delicious cream soup.

6 sprigs parsley	1½ cups milk
2 pounds cauliflower	Salt to taste
6 cups chicken stock (see index)	Garlic croutons

Rinse and clean parsley, remove leaves, and mince; set aside.

Place the cauliflower in a large pot ¼ full with water. Bring to a boil, reduce heat to medium, and cook for 15-20 minutes, until tender. Drain and discard green leaves and liquid. Place cooked cauliflower in blender with 1 cup of chicken broth and blend.

In the large pot, bring the remaining chicken stock to a boil, add the ground cauliflower, and let simmer 15 minutes. Just before serving add the milk and let it come to a boil. Add salt to taste. Serve immediately. Garnish with minced parsley and croutons. Serves 6.

CREMA DE CHAMPIÑONES
(Cream of Mushroom Soup)

¾ lb. small mushrooms	2 tbsp. butter or margarine
Water to cover	Salt to taste
4 cups milk	

Clean mushrooms; remove stems. Put mushrooms in a heavy pot covered with water and bring to a boil. Simmer for 10 minutes covered, remove from heat, and drain water. Place half of the mushrooms with half of the milk in blender and puree; set aside. Chop the remaining mushrooms and set aside. Heat butter or margarine in a dutch oven and fry remaining mushrooms for 5 minutes over low heat. Add the puree and the remaining milk and salt. Let come to a boil, reduce heat, and simmer 15 minutes on low heat. Serves 6.

CREMA DE ELOTE
(Cream of Corn Soup)

This is a simple and easy cream soup to prepare.

4 cups cooked corn kernels　　　　**2 cups milk**
5 cups beef stock (see index)　　　**Salt and pepper to taste**

Place 3 cups corn kernels in blender and grind with 1 cup beef stock. Transfer to large soup pot and bring to a boil. Add remaining beef stock, milk, and corn. Let simmer 5-8 minutes. Add salt and pepper to taste. Serve immediately. Serves 6.

CREMA DE CHÍCHAROS FRESCOS
(Cream of Fresh Pea Soup)

Fresh peas in Mexico are unusually tasty and available all year, making it a very popular vegetable. This fresh pea cream soup is delicious.

2 carrots　　　　　　　　　　　　　**3 tbsp. butter or margarine**
4 cups fresh or frozen peas (not　　**1 cup ham, finely diced**
**　canned)**　　　　　　　　　　　　　**Salt to taste**
4 cups milk

Peel and finely dice carrots. In a small pan, bring 2 cups water to a boil. Transfer carrots to pot, reduce heat, and simmer carrots for 10 minutes.

In another small pan, simmer peas for 15 minutes, exactly as you did the carrots. Remove cooked peas from stove and let cool. In a blender, puree the peas with ½ cup milk.

In a heavy soup pot, heat butter or margarine and brown diced ham, about 5 minutes. Transfer puree to ham and add remaining m.lk and carrots. Reduce heat and let simmer for 15 minutes, stirring occasionally. Adjust salt. Serves 6.

CHAPTER 9
RICE AND PASTA

Most Mexicans take two hours for lunch (from 1:00 to 3:00 P.M.), the principal meal of the day. They either go home to have lunch or have their lunch at eateries or restaurants where the main menu is the so-called *comida comercial* (commercial lunch), which is affordable for their sometimes meager pockets.

Generally lunch consists of three or four courses, plus dessert and coffee. Aside from the varied soups there is always the option of a plate of *sopa seca* (rice or pasta). In many households and restaurants the rice or pasta is served as one of the main courses by itself, not as a side dish.

ARROZ MEXICANO
(Mexican Rice)

3 cups long grain rice
¼ onion
1 tomato
1 cup peas fresh or frozen
  (not canned)
2 carrots

¼ cup cilantro
6 cups chicken stock (see index)
¼ cup corn oil
2 hard-boiled eggs, sliced in rounds
12 pickled jalapeño or serrano
  chilies

Place raw rice in a colander and run tap water over rice to remove excess starch. Dry with a paper towel and place rice to one side for later use.

Chop onion. Chop tomato. Peel and dice carrots. Rinse and chop cilantro.

Bring chicken stock to a boil. In a heavy frying pan on medium, heat the oil and fry the rice with the onion until the rice jumps around in the pan (about 5 minutes). Now add the tomato and sauté stirring constantly for 3 to 4 minutes. Pour boiling chicken stock over rice; let come to a boil. Add peas, carrots, and cilantro. Reduce heat to low and let simmer covered (do not uncover) for 20 minutes. Turn heat off, but let sit on burner for 10 minutes so the rice will become fluffy. Garnish with sliced eggs and pickled chilies. Serves 6.

ARROZ BLANCO
(White Rice)

3 cups long grain rice
6 cups chicken stock (see index)

¼ cup corn oil
Salt to taste

Rinse rice.

Bring chicken stock to a boil. In a heavy frying pan on medium, heat the oil and fry the rice until it jumps around in the pan (about 5 minutes). Pour boiling chicken stock over rice; let come to a boil. Reduce heat to low and let simmer covered (do not uncover) for 20 minutes. Turn heat off, but let sit on burner for 10 minutes so the rice will become fluffy. Adjust salt. Serves 6.

ARROZ CON CAMARONES
(Rice with Shrimp)

36 medium fresh shrimp
1 tsp. red wine vinegar
1 medium white onion
1 red bell pepper
1 cup fresh or frozen peas
   (not canned)

6 cups water
¼ cup corn oil
3 cups long grain rice

To shell shrimp, just push the shell with your thumb and forefinger and it will come off. Remove tail. With a sharp knife cut along the curve in the body and remove the back vein. Rinse shrimp under cool water. Transfer shrimp to a mixing bowl filled with ice-cold water and then add the vinegar. Place bowl in the refrigerator for 10 minutes.

Mince onion; set aside. Slice red bell pepper in strips, discard stem and seeds, and set aside. Bring to a boil the 6 cups water and turn heat to warm until ready to use for rice.

Remove shrimp from refrigerator and discard water. Drain chilled shrimp on paper towels.

In a large heavy frying pan, heat oil and sauté rice over medium heat, stirring frequently for 3 minutes. Add red bell pepper strips and onion and continue frying until rice jumps around in pan. Pour the 6 cups hot water over rice, add peas, let come to a boil, and reduce heat. Let cook covered for 10 minutes. Uncover, add shrimp, and let cook covered for 20 minutes. At this point, uncover to see that all the liquid is evaporated. Turn heat off and let rice sit on burner for 10 minutes covered — it will continue to become fluffy. Do not uncover. Serves 6.

ARROZ VERDE
(Green Rice)

3 cups rice
4 poblano chilies
6 cups boiling chicken stock
  (see index)

¼ onion
2 cloves garlic
1 cup corn kernels
¼ cup corn oil

Rinse rice.

On a comal roast the poblano or California chilies until the skins blister. Place these chilies in a cellophane bag and let sweat for 10 minutes. Remove from bag and peel skins as best you can. Remove stem from each chili and remove seeds; cut chili in strips.

In a blender with 1 cup of the chicken stock, grind ½ of the chili strips with the stock. Leave ½ of the strips intact.

Chop onion. Mince garlic.

Add the chicken stock in the blender with the ground poblano chilies to the regular chicken stock. It will turn a pale green color. Bring chicken stock to a boil. In a heavy frying pan on medium, heat the oil and fry the rice with the onion and remaining chili strips until the rice jumps around in the pan (about 5 minutes). Pour boiling chicken stock over rice. At this point, add corn and garlic and let come to a boil. Reduce heat to low and let simmer covered (do not uncover) for 20 minutes. Turn heat off, but let sit on burner for 10 minutes so the rice will become fluffy. Serves 6.

ARROZ CON POLLO
(Rice with Chicken)

3 cups long grain rice
6 chicken legs with thighs
¼ onion
1 potato
1 cup peas, fresh or frozen
  (not canned)

½ cup corn kernels
¼ cup cilantro, chopped
6 cups chicken stock (see index)
¼ cup corn oil
Salt to taste

Rinse rice.

In a heavy frying pan, brown chicken pieces. Remove them to a platter once they are browned.

Chop onion. Peel potato and chop in cubes.

Bring chicken stock to a boil. In a heavy frying pan on medium, heat the oil and fry the rice with the onion until the rice jumps around in the pan (about 5 minutes). Pour boiling chicken stock over rice. At this point, add the potato, peas, corn, cilantro, and chicken pieces; let come to a boil. Reduce heat to low and let simmer covered (do not uncover) for 20 minutes. Turn heat off, but let sit on burner for 10 minutes so the rice will become fluffy. Adjust salt. Serves 6.

ARROZ CON RAJAS Y QUESO
(Rice with Rajas and Cheese)

When someone refers to ''rajas'' in Mexican cuisine, they generally mean strips of poblano chili, but rajas can be any other pepper sliced into strips. This rice recipe with rajas is a good idea for a small party.

6 poblano or California chilies
3 cups long grain rice
6 cups chicken stock (see index)
Salt to taste
¼ cup corn oil

2 cups grated Manchego or
   Jack cheese
¼ cup milk
1 cup plain yogurt

On a comal roast the poblano or California chilies until the skins blister. Place these chilies in a cellophane bag and let sweat for 10 minutes. Remove from bag and peel skins as best you can. Remove stem from each chili and remove seeds. Cut in strips. Set aside for later use.

Rinse rice.

Bring chicken stock to a boil. In a heavy frying pan on medium, heat the oil and fry the rice until it jumps around in the pan (about 5 minutes). Pour boiling chicken stock over rice; let come to a boil. Reduce heat to low and let simmer covered (do not uncover) for 20 minutes. Turn heat off, but let sit on burner for 10 minutes so the rice will become fluffy.

With a beater, mix the milk into the yogurt.

In an earthenware casserole, place a layer of rice, topped with some rajas, some cream mixture, and grated cheese. Repeat this in the same order; the last layer should be cheese. Cover the casserole and place in oven at 375 degrees F (190 degrees C) for 25 minutes. Serve immediately. Serves 6.

Variation: Add 1 cup of ham sliced in strips.

PAELLA

Saffron is the dried stigmas (filaments) of an ancient member of the crocus family described as the world's most costly spice. Each *Crocus sativus* blossom only yields three delicate, orange-colored stigmas, which must be picked by hand. It takes more than 225,000 of them to make a pound. The good news is that saffron goes a long way. It is used to achieve a rich, golden color and exotic flavor. Saffron is used as a seasoning for many foods, especially in Spain. There are so many Spanish immigrants in Mexico that this Spanish paella recipe has been included as a necessary Mexican Sunday meal.

1 1½-lb. lobster	1 red bell pepper
½ lb. pork, in 1-inch cubes	6 canned artichoke hearts
½ lb. beef, in very small pieces	½ cup peas, fresh or frozen (not
1 small chicken, in pieces	canned)
½ lb. smoked ham, in thin strips	3 cups long grain rice
½ lb. medium shrimp	½ tsp. saffron stigmas
1 tsp. red wine vinegar	¼ cup olive oil
1½ dozen clams	2 nutcrackers (to remove meat from
1 small onion	lobster easily)
3 cloves garlic	6 seafood forks

Never cook a dead lobster. The larger the lobster the more likely it is to be tough. The small lobster is the most tender and delicious. The lobster should be cooked with the legs and tail tied to prevent it from breaking and losing blood when agitated.

In a large covered pot, bring 3 quarts of water and about 3 tablespoons of salt to a full boil. Grasp lobster by the back and plunge head first into the water. Bring water to another boil, cover, reduce heat, and simmer for 5 minutes for the first pound, 3 minutes for each additional pound. Drain hot water from lobster and then cover lobster with cold water to chill. Drain again and place lobster shell-side down on a cutting board.

Slit the bony membrane on the underside of the tail. The intestinal vein is then removed and discarded. Cut the body of the lobster lengthwise, but not through the shell. Remove and discard the intestinal vein running lengthwise through the center of the body. Remove and discard stomach (a small sac which lies in the head) and the lungs (which lie in the upper body cavity, between meat and shell). The green liver and coral (red roe) should be discarded. Leave the lobster whole. Drain on paper towels and place on a platter in refrigerator until ready to use.

In a heavy frying pan, brown the pork pieces, cover, and let cook 20 minutes more. Remove pork to an oven-proof deep casserole in warm oven. Brown beef in same frying pan, cover, and let cook 20 minutes more. Place in casserole already in oven with pork to keep warm. Brown the chicken, cover, and let cook 10-15 minutes. Place chicken in warm oven with pork and beef. Brown ham for 5 minutes then add to the casserole in warm oven, until ready to use.

Shell shrimp — just push the shell with your thumb and forefinger and it will come off. Leave tail intact. With a sharp knife cut along the curve in the body and remove the back vein. Rinse shrimp under cool water. Transfer shrimp to a mixing bowl filled with ice-cold water and then add the red wine vinegar and place in the refrigerator until ready to use.

Clams decompose rapidly after they are dead; that is why they are cooked when they are still alive. Clams that do not open when cooked should be discarded. Scrub clams with a hard brush to remove sand particles. Dry on paper towels and place in refrigerator until ready to use.

Finely chop onion; set aside. Mince garlic and set aside. Slice red bell pepper in strips; set aside. Open can of artichoke hearts and drain liquid. Have peas handy for quick use.

Rinse rice.

You are now ready to prepare paella. When cooking the paella, the burner should cover the whole bottom of the pan. The special pan for cooking paella is a shallow iron pan with a flat bottom, sloping sides, and a handle at each side. If this type of pan is not available, use a shallow frying pan with sloping edges.

In a blender with ½ cup warm water, place the saffron stigmas and let stand for about 3 minutes. Then turn blender on to grind until the water turns yellow.

Bring 5½ cups water to a boil (to use with rice).

In the paella pan heat the oil and brown the onion, garlic, and rice until the rice is jumping around in the oil. Add the bell pepper. Add the artichoke hearts and peas. Add boiling water to rice, reduce heat, and add saffron water from blender. Cover and let rice simmer 10 minutes on low heat. Uncover rice and quickly add to the rice the meat casserole that is in the oven, and the shrimp and clams. Cover and cook about 15 minutes more on lowest heat.

Place lobster on casserole dish in oven.

Turn heat off of rice mixture and let sit on burner 15 minutes more so all the liquid will be absorbed.

In a large earthenware dish, place the paella and top with the lobster. Serve immediately with lots of napkins, the nutcrackers, and seafood forks. Serves 6.

FIDEOS EN JITOMATE
(Vermicelli Noodles)

This is a "dry soup."

¼ cup corn oil
4 oz. vermicelli twists
2 tomatoes
¼ small onion

1 clove garlic
8 cups chicken stock (see index)
Salt and pepper to taste
1 cup Parmesan cheese, grated

In a heavy soup pan on low heat, warm oil and fry the vermicelli twists, being careful not to overbrown. Drain on paper towels; set aside. In a blender, grind the tomatoes, onion, and garlic. Fry the tomato mixture in the same soup pan for 5 minutes. Pour in chicken stock and season with salt and pepper to taste. Bring to a boil, add drained vermicelli, and let simmer over low heat 20 or 25 minutes, until pasta is cooked and dry. Add cheese. Serves 6.

CHAPTER 10
POULTRY

Neither the native Aztecs nor the other Indian civilizations down south or the nomadic tribes of hunters and gatherers in the Central and South American continent knew about chickens (hens). Chickens were taken to Latin America by the Spanish conquistadors and became a part of every household, whether of the *casa de hacienda* (country estate house) or of the humble peasant hut. Nowadays, chicken in Mexico is eaten at the same volume as in the U.S., but it is more expensive than beef. The Aztecs did have turkeys (*guajolotes* in Mexico) and partridges, which were usually eaten at ceremonies. Nowadays the turkey, especially with mole, is eaten at family celebrations.

RECETA BÁSICA PARA
POLLO DESHEBRADO
(Basic Recipe for Shredded Chicken)

Shredded chicken is used in many Mexican recipes.

5 cups water	**2 bay leaves**
6 chicken breasts	**¼ tsp. cumin**
1 white onion, whole	**⅛ tsp. oregano**
6 cloves garlic, whole	**Salt to taste**

In a large pot, boil the water. Add chicken breasts, whole onion, garlic, bay leaves, cumin, and oregano; cover the pot. Let the chicken boil for 5 minutes, reduce heat to low, and let simmer for 35 to 45 minutes, or until the chicken is tender. Adjust salt. Remove chicken with a slotted spoon. Discard the onion, garlic, and bay leaves. (Save chicken stock in a container to use in another recipe such as Mexican rice.) Shred the cooked chicken. Serves 6.

TACOS DE POLLO
(Chicken Tacos)

1 basic recipe for shredded chicken (see previous recipe)	**24 corn tortillas**
	½ cup corn oil
1 recipe ranch sauce (see opposite page)	

Before you begin to make tacos, prepare basic recipes for shredded chicken and ranch sauce.

Heat griddle on medium heat and warm tortillas. Fill each with about 3 tablespoons of shredded chicken. Roll filled tortillas closed, into tacos. Secure them with wooden picks if desired, or lean a heavy metal spoon on top of first few tacos to keep them closed. Heat oil in heavy frying pan and fry each taco, turning to fry all sides. Serve immediately. Accompany with ranch sauce. Makes 24 tacos.

TOSTADAS COMPUESTAS
(Chicken Tostadas)

Although *tostada* in many a Latin country means toasted bread, in Mexico tostadas are made by frying a tortilla to a crisp and garnishing it. Tostadas are tempting to the most discriminating palate. Humble women in Mexico offering tostadas to hungry passers-by find that as soon as the tostada is made it is gone. Tostadas are a successful item on any fonda's menu. They are easy to make for entertaining.

1 basic recipe for shredded chicken (see opposite page)
1 recipe refried beans (see index)
1 recipe green tomatillo sauce (see index)
1 head Romaine lettuce
1 bunch radishes
1 large white onion
2 cups Manchego or Jack cheese, grated
2 Haas avocados
24 corn tortillas
½ cup corn oil
1 cup plain yogurt

Before you begin to make tostadas make recipes of shredded chicken, refried beans, and green tomatillo sauce.

Rinse the lettuce and the radishes. Slice the lettuce in small pieces and cut the radishes in rounds. Slice onion in rounds. Slice the avocados. Stir the yogurt until softened and place in a serving dish.

You are now ready for the preparation of the tostadas. Fry the tortillas in oil until crisp, drain on paper towels, and keep warm in the oven. Spread these toasted tortillas (now you know why they are called "tostadas") with refried beans and cover with a generous portion of shredded chicken, a splash of green salsa, some yogurt, shredded cheese, lettuce pieces, avocado slices, some radishes, and onion slices. Offer extra salsa as a garnish. This is definitely fun finger food. Serves 6.

POLLO EN SALSA DE ALMENDRA
(Chicken in Almond Sauce)

The almonds give this sauce a special flavor and are used as a thickening agent.

5-6 cups water
6 chicken breasts, cut in half
1 ½ onions
4 cloves garlic, minced
¼ tsp. thyme, dried
3 tomatoes, unpeeled
1 cup almonds, with skins
¼ cup bread crumbs

¼ cup corn oil
1 cup white wine
25 whole green olives
Salt and pepper to taste
1 can of jalapeño or serrano chilies
** to taste**
24 corn tortillas

In a large heavy pot, bring the water to a boil, add chicken breasts, 1 whole onion, ½ of the minced garlic, and thyme. Reduce heat and let simmer 45-50 minutes until chicken is tender. Remove chicken from stock, place in an oven-proof dish, and keep warm in oven. Discard onion from stock; set stock aside.

On a griddle, roast the tomatoes, ½ onion (in quarters), remaining garlic, and almonds on low heat, being careful not to burn. In blender grind the tomatoes, onion, garlic, and almonds, with 1 cup cooled chicken stock and bread crumbs.

Heat oil in heavy frying pan and sauté the tomato-almond mixture until it forms a paste, about 5 minutes. Add 4 to 5 cups of the remaining chicken stock and let simmer for 1 hour on low heat until the sauce thickens, stirring occasionally. Add the white wine and the olives to the almond sauce and let cook 30 minutes again on low heat, stirring frequently to prevent sauce from sticking to pan. Add salt and pepper to taste.

Remove chicken from oven, place on a serving platter, and pour almond sauce over the warmed chicken. Garnish with the chilies. Serve warm with plenty of corn tortillas. Serves 6.

POLLO MANCHAMANTELES
(Messy-Tablecloth Chicken)

Don't use your favorite tablecloth when you serve this one.

7 cups water
6 chicken breasts, split in half
1½ white onions
4 cloves garlic, minced
2 ancho chilies
1 large sweet potato
¼ cup corn oil
4 tbsp. peanuts, shelled and peeled
2 tomatoes, unpeeled

1 tbsp. red wine vinegar
1 tsp. sugar
2 green apples
1 plantain
12 prunes, dried
2 slices fresh pineapple, cut into
   large cubes
24 corn tortillas

In a large heavy pot bring the water to a boil and add chicken breasts, 1 whole onion, and 2 minced garlic cloves. Reduce heat and let simmer for 45-50 minutes, until chicken is tender. Remove chicken from stock, place on an oven-proof dish, and keep warm. Discard whole onion. Reserve stock.

Rinse the ancho chilies under cold running water and then place them in a bowl of water until they are soft and pliable. With a slotted spoon, remove chilies from the water, and discard the veins, seeds, and stems. Drain.

Peel the sweet potato, cut it in quarters, and place in a medium pan with boiling water. Reduce heat and let simmer for 20-25 minutes until tender when a fork is inserted. Drain water; set aside.

In a heavy frying pan heat oil and fry the remaining ½ onion, 2 cloves garlic, and peanuts, being careful not to burn. When they are browned, with a spatula remove them from the frying pan and place in blender. Grind with tomatoes and chilies. Return the sauce to the frying pan and simmer for 2 minutes. Add half of the stock and all of the vinegar and sugar.

Peel and core the apples; chop in small pieces. Peel and chop the plantain in small pieces. Add the sweet potatoes and all the fruits to the tomato-peanut sauce.

Remove the chicken from the warm oven and place on serving platter. Pour the fruit sauce over the chicken and serve immediately with plenty of warm tortillas. Serves 6.

POLLO CON ARROZ DE AZAFRÁN
(Chicken with Saffron Rice)

The taste and natural color that the saffron gives to this rice is unequaled.

3 whole chicken breasts, halved
¼ cup corn oil
Salt to taste
1 red bell pepper
4 cups chicken stock (see index)
3 cups long grain rice

⅓ tsp. saffron
½ cup frozen peas
12 pearl onions, sliced
2 marinated serrano chilies, sliced
   (see Traditional Pickled Chilies)

In a heavy frying pan, fry the chicken in oil until browned. Salt to taste. Remove chicken to a glass casserole dish and place in the oven on warm until ready to use. Slice the red bell pepper into thin strips, and fry in the same frying pan used to fry the chicken; set aside. Rinse frying pan for the next use.

Heat chicken stock.

In a heavy frying pan, fry the rice until browned. (It does not necessarily have to look brown; you can tell the rice has been browned enough when rice starts to jump or, rather, "move" around in pan.) Add hot chicken stock, fried bell pepper, and saffron. Gently stir saffron into rice, then add frozen peas and browned chicken. Leave covered and cook over low heat for 20 minutes. Remove cover to see if rice is dry. If not, cook another 5 minutes covered. Once dry, turn heat off and leave covered on stove for 15 minutes for rice to become fluffy. Fry pearl onions and serrano chilies in a frying pan. Garnish chicken and rice with fried pearl onions and serrano chilies. Serves 6.

POLLO AL AJILLO
(Chicken in Garlic)

The very first time we tried this delicious chicken was in a tiny *rosticeria* ("take-out" for roasted chickens) in Colonia Anzures in Mexico City, where there was a long line of people waiting for their roasted chicken to finish cooking. The roasted chickens were placed in sealed cellophane bags "to go" and customers were given a small sealed cellophane bag of marinated jalapeño chilies to take with them. The proprietor was continually roasting more chickens to fulfill the demand — and it seemed to be an endless task. We asked the owner to explain his technique, which we share here. Since few homes have a rotating roaster of this type, we have recreated his recipe for a home oven. If you have a rotating roaster or a barbecue try your hand at this marinated chicken.

2- to 3-lb. broiler-fryers, split	**1 jar marinated jalapeño chilies**
12 cloves garlic	**(see Traditional Pickled Chilies)**
¼ cup corn oil	**24 corn tortillas**

Rinse the chicken under cold running water, pat dry with paper towels, and set aside. Mince garlic cloves. Rub chicken with oil and then rub with the minced garlic. Place prepared chicken in a cellophane bag in the refrigerator at least 8 hours, or overnight.

Heat oven to 450 degrees F (232 degrees C). Bake chicken uncovered for 10 minutes. Baste with drippings. Reduce heat to 350 degrees F (176 degrees C); cover and bake an additional 45 minutes, or until tender. You can make it into taquitos using the chilies and tortillas. Serves 6.

GUISADO DE POLLO A LA CERVEZA
(Chicken Stew in Beer)

The Mexicans like to cook with beer, and if you try this recipe you will see why.

3 chicken breasts	**½ onion**
3 chicken legs	**12 mushrooms**
3 chicken thighs	**1 (12 oz.) beer**
¼ cup corn oil	**12 green olives**
2 carrots	**1 tsp. pequín chili, ground**
3 medium potatoes	**Salt and pepper to taste**

In a heavy soup pot, fry the pieces of chicken in oil until they are browned. Slice the carrots in rounds, peel and halve the potatoes, and set aside. Mince the onion. Clean and halve the mushrooms. Add the minced onion and mushrooms to the browned chicken and sauté for 2-3 minutes more. Add the beer. When it comes to a boil add the carrots, potatoes, and olives. Cover and let simmer for 25 minutes. Add the ground pequín chili and simmer for another 15 minutes on medium heat until ingredients are tender. Add salt and pepper to taste. Serves 6.

POLLOS BORRACHOS
(Drunken Chickens)

Obviously, the reason for the name of this dish is the use of wine, as well as an over-active imagination.

2 large tomatoes	¼ cup corn oil
¼ cup chopped onion	¼ tsp. thyme, dried
2 cloves garlic	1 cup dried ham
2 sprigs parsley	4 cups red wine or sherry
2 (3 lb. each) broiler-fryers, split	Salt and pepper to taste

Keeping ingredients separate, finely chop tomatoes and mince garlic. Rinse parsley and mince. In a heavy frying pan fry chicken in oil for about 10-15 minutes until brown on all sides. Add chopped onion and garlic and sauté 2-3 minutes more. Then add tomatoes, thyme, and parsley and simmer for 20 minutes.

Slice the dried ham in strips and add to chicken; simmer 10 more minutes. Add red wine and cook for 15 minutes more. Season with salt and pepper to taste. Serves 6.

POLLO A LA AZTECA
(Chicken Aztec Style)

Generally when you hear the name "Aztec" over and over in different recipes you can be sure that it will use as a main ingredient corn or corn tortillas.

1 Basic Recipe for Shredded Chicken (see index)	¼ cup corn oil
4 medium tomatoes	Salt to taste
6 garlic cloves	12 corn tortillas
¼ onion	2 cups Manchego or Jack cheese, shredded
1 to 2 chipotle chilies (canned, smoked)	

First, prepare shredded chicken.

In a blender, grind the tomatoes, garlic, onion, and chipotle chili until they form a sauce. Heat oil in heavy frying pan. Simmer the sauce in it for about 10 minutes. Adjust salt.

Preheat oven to 350 degrees F (176 degrees C).

Heat the corn tortillas on a hot griddle. Dip the warmed tortillas in the sauce and put each dipped tortilla in an oven-proof 8-inch by 18-inch casserole. Fill each dipped tortilla with 4 to 5 tablespoons of shredded chicken and fold in half. When you are finished cover with remaining sauce. Top with shredded cheese. Place in oven until cheese melts. Serve warm from oven. Serves 6.

CHILAQUILES CON POLLO
(Chilaquiles with Chicken)

Chilaquiles are made with day-old hard tortillas, cut in pie shapes and fried until crisp (called "totopos" at this point), then some ranch sauce is poured over them.

1 Basic Recipe for Shredded Chicken (see index)
1 recipe ranch sauce (see index)
12 tortillas
½ cup corn oil

1½ cups plain yogurt, slightly stirred
2 cups Manchego or Jack cheese, grated

First prepare shredded chicken and ranch sauce.

Cut tortillas in pie-shaped pieces. Fry the tortilla pieces in oil in frying pan until crispy, drain on paper towels, and set aside.

Heat oven to 325 F (162 degrees C).

Grease an oven-proof earthenware casserole; place a layer of the chicken, a layer of the totopos, and top with the ranch sauce, stirred yogurt, and grated cheese. Repeat until all ingredients are used. Sprinkle remaining grated cheese on top. Place in oven for 15 minutes, or until the casserole is hot and bubbly. Serves 6.

Variation: Prepare rajas from poblano chilies and add to the casserole alternately in layers with the chicken and totopos.

AUTENTICO MOLE ESTILO PUEBLA
(Authentic Mole Puebla Style)

Mole is a dish served at important family celebrations and we highly recommend it to you. Every Mexican cook thinks she has the secret to the best mole. Some cooks say that mole needs the smoked flavor of the fiery chipotle chili, while others argue that it does not. Some say a handful of roasted peanuts makes or breaks the mole and others prefer to use almonds. So the cook best avoids arguments by referring mysteriously to her "secret mole recipe." The real secret to a great mole is a good stock.

6 mulato chilies	**½ corn tortilla**
4 ancho chilies	**½ onion**
2 pasilla chilies	**6 cloves garlic**
2 smoked chipotle chilies, canned	**½ tsp. red wine vinegar**
¾ cup vegetable shortening	**2 oz. Mexican chocolate bar (it is**
¼ cup sesame seeds	**made with cinnamon)**
1 cup almonds	**1 tbsp. sugar**
¼ cup raisins	**1 tsp. salt**
¼ ripe banana	**1 (8 to 9 lb.) turkey**
¼ ground cinnamon	**6 tsp. sesame seeds**
3 medium tomatoes, roasted	**24 fresh corn tortillas**

Rinse the dried mulato, ancho and pasilla chilies under cold running water, place them in a bowl immersed with water overnight. The next morning, when they are soft, grind the chilies in a blender with ¼ cup of the water used to soak them in and the chipotle chilies until a smooth paste forms and the pieces of chili are finely ground. If paste is too thick add more water, 2 tablespoons at a time. Transfer paste to a bowl, and with an electric mixer on medium-low speed, beat in vegetable shortening until a smooth paste forms. Transfer paste back to blender with ½ cup liquid and grind paste with the ¼ cup sesame seeds, almonds, raisins, banana, cinnamon, tomatoes, ½ tortilla, onion, garlic, and vinegar until a smooth paste forms. Sauté the paste about 5 minutes, stirring constantly so it will not stick to the bottom of the pan. Mix in Mexican chocolate, sugar, and salt and continue cooking until the paste is smooth, about 5 minutes more. If the mole paste is too thick add more liquid.

Have your butcher cut turkey into pieces. In a large heavy pot, brown turkey on all sides. Pour 8 cups boiling water over turkey and let boil for 1 minute. Reduce heat and let simmer 45 minutes. Mix in mole paste and continue simmering until mole sauce thickens like a gravy (if sauce gets too thick add more liquid, ¼ cup at a time), about 30 minutes.

Heat oven to 350 degrees F (176 degrees C). On a cookie sheet roast the 6 teaspoons sesame seeds for about 10 minutes. Remove from oven and set aside.

On individual serving plates, place some turkey in mole sauce garnished with roasted sesame seeds and accompany with Mexican rice and plenty of tortillas. Serves 6.

TACOS DE POLLO CON MOLE
(Chicken-Mole Tacos)

The flavor of mole makes these tacos very delicious.

1 Basic Recipe for Shredded
   Chicken (see index)
¼ cup mole Doña María paste
1 tomato

1 cup chicken stock
Salt to taste
24 corn tortillas
½ cup corn oil

Heat oven to 450 degrees F (232 degrees C).

Prepare shredded chicken before making the tacos.

Place mole paste in blender with tomato and chicken stock and grind until a smooth paste forms. In a heavy saucepan simmer this sauce until it thickens, about 10-15 minutes. Adjust salt. Set aside.

Dip shredded chicken in the mole sauce. Warm tortillas on a hot griddle and place in a napkin to keep warm. Place 3 tablespoons of chicken on each warmed tortilla. Roll closed with the seam side down. Secure with a wooden pick if desired. Heat oil in heavy frying pan and fry each taco in the oil, turning to fry all sides. Serve immediately. Serves 6.

MOLE PREPARADO CON POLLO
(Ready-Made Chicken Mole)

Even the best cooks in Mexico have to confess that they use ready-made mole paste to make their ''secret'' recipe. There are a few exceptions among indigenous women who still prefer to grind the three main dry chili pods and create their own mole paste, but even the ultra-traditional use the modern blender instead of the stone metate to grind. In any event, we have provided you with the recipe for Authentic Mole Puebla Style in case you should want to experience making your own paste. Our favorite method of making mole is the ready-made paste. They sell these mole pastes in bulk now in most grocery stores in Mexico and the U.S. The brand of mole paste we recommend is called Doña María and it has been a favorite among Mexican cooks for more than thirty years. There is no need to add additional chili pods or chocolate to this mole paste. It should be easy for your grocer to order it. However, another brand can safely be substituted.

3 chicken breasts, halved	1 corn tortilla
6 chicken legs	1 chipotle chili, canned
6 chicken thighs	Salt and pepper to taste
6 cups boiling water	¼ cup roasted sesame seeds (see
1 onion, whole	Authentic Mole Puebla Style)
2 cloves garlic, whole	¼ cup raisins
½ onion	1 cup Doña María mole paste
2 cloves garlic	¼ cup corn oil
½ cup almonds	¼ cup roasted sesame seeds for
3 tomatoes	garnish
¼ banana	24 fresh corn tortillas

In a dutch oven, brown chicken pieces on all sides. Add the boiling water, whole onion, and 2 whole garlics. Bring to a boil for 1 minute, reduce heat, and let simmer 20-25 minutes. When chicken is tender, drain with a slotted spoon and place chicken on an oven-proof platter in oven on warm until ready to use. When chicken stock is cool, pour it into a glass bowl to free the dutch oven for later use; set aside.

On a comal or griddle roast the ½ onion, 2 garlic cloves, almonds and tomatoes turning frequently. As each ingredient is roasted place it in the blender with banana, tortilla, chipotle chili, salt, and pepper. In addition, add ¼ cup sesame seeds and the raisins to the blender. Grind these ingredients with 1 cup of chicken stock. Add the mole paste to the blender and grind for 3 minutes more until a paste is formed. (You should not discard the oil from the mole paste. Once your mole is fully prepared, let the sauce cool. The oil will rise, and you can then remove it from the sauce.)

Heat oil in the dutch oven and fry this paste for about 5 minutes over low heat. Then add the remaining chicken stock to the paste and let simmer until it thickens to a gravy consistency. Place warmed chicken on serving platter and smother with the mole sauce. Sprinkle with the roasted sesame seeds. Accompany with corn tortillas. Serves 6.

MOLE LIGERO SUPREMO CON POLLO
(Supreme Light Mole with Chicken)

This mole is as simple to make as a roasted salsa with mole paste added. The secret is a rich chicken or turkey stock. We call it "light mole" because it does not have anything other than the roasted tomato sauce and the mole paste with the chicken stock.

3 chicken breasts, halved	**3 tomatoes**
6 chicken legs	**1 chipotle chili, canned**
6 chicken thighs	**Salt and pepper to taste**
6 cups boiling water	**1 cup Doña María mole paste**
1 onion, whole	**½ cup roasted sesame seeds (see**
2 cloves garlic, whole	**Authentic Mole Puebla Style)**
½ onion	**24 fresh corn tortillas**
2 cloves garlic	

In a dutch oven, brown chicken pieces on all sides. Add the boiling water, whole onion, and 2 whole garlics. Bring to a boil for 1 minute, reduce heat, and let simmer 20-25 minutes. When chicken is tender, drain with a slotted spoon and place chicken on an oven-proof platter in oven on warm until ready to use. When chicken stock is cool, pour it into a glass bowl to free the dutch oven for later use; set aside.

On a comal or griddle roast the ½ onion, 2 cloves garlic, and tomatoes, turning frequently. As each ingredient is roasted place it in the blender with the chipotle chili, salt, and pepper. Grind these ingredients with 1 cup of chicken stock. Add the mole paste to the blender and grind for 3 minutes more until a paste is formed.

In the dutch oven fry this paste for about 5 minutes over low heat. Then add the remaining chicken stock to the paste and let simmer until it thickens to a gravy consistency. Let sauce cool so oils will rise; once cool remove oil from top of sauce. Rewarm sauce. Place warmed chicken on serving platter and smother with the mole sauce. Sprinkle with the roasted sesame seeds. Accompany with corn tortillas. Serves 6.

ENCHILADAS DE POLLO DE MOLE
(Chicken Enchiladas with Mole Sauce)

The authentic method of making enchiladas is to fry the tortillas (one at a time) 30 seconds on both sides, dip the fried tortillas once in a bowl of sauce or mole, transfer to another plate to fill with a favorite filling, and roll closed. Transfer to a rectangle casserole, pour remaining sauce and grated cheese on top, and bake in 375 degree F (191 degree C) oven for 10 minutes. (Sometimes they are not even baked in the oven.) Serve immediately garnished with sliced lettuce, radishes, and sour cream.

We hope you enjoy cooking these enchiladas because your family is going to request them over and over again, if they are like our family.

**1 Basic Recipe for Shredded
  Chicken (see index)
2 tomatoes
½ onion
2 cloves garlic
4 cups chicken stock (see index)**

**1 cup Doña María mole paste
1 chipotle chili
24 corn tortillas
¼ cup corn oil
¼ cup roasted sesame seeds (see
  Authentic Mole Puebla Style)**

First, prepare the shredded chicken.

On a hot griddle over medium heat roast the tomatoes, onion and garlic. Place roasted ingredients in blender and grind until a paste is formed. Add 1 cup cooled chicken stock and mole paste, as well as chipotle chili, and grind until paste is smooth; set aside. Return this sauce to a heavy pot and bring to a boil, stirring frequently. Add 3 cups chicken stock and let simmer for 15-20 minutes until sauce thickens. Pour ½ cup of this mole sauce on the shredded chicken; set aside again for later use.

Heat oven to 350 degrees F (176 degrees C).

Warm tortillas on comal or griddle; place warmed tortillas in a napkin to keep warm. In a heavy frying pan, fry each tortilla in oil and begin filling with shredded chicken. Roll closed seam side down and place in a casserole. Pour mole sauce over filled tortillas and place in oven for 15 minutes. Remove enchiladas from oven and sprinkle with sesame seeds. Serve immediately. Serves 6.

ENCHILADAS DE POLLO
EN SALSA DE TOMATILLO
(Chicken Enchiladas in Tomatillo Sauce)

Enchiladas are no more than filled tortillas which are closed, fried, and smothered in different sauces. We know you will enjoy making them as much as eating them once they become a part of your regular recipes.

1 Basic Recipe for Shredded Chicken (see index)
1 recipe green tomatillo sauce (see index)
24 corn tortillas
¼ cup corn oil

1 cup Manchego or Jack cheese, grated
1 Romaine lettuce
2 avocados, sliced
12 radishes
½ cup plain yogurt

First prepare the shredded chicken and the green tomatillo sauce.

Preheat oven to 350 degrees F (176 degrees C).

Heat tortillas on a hot griddle and transfer to napkin-lined basket to keep warm. Heat oil in a heavy frying pan on medium heat. Fry the tortillas, about 30 seconds on each side, drain them on paper towels, and fill with shredded chicken. Roll closed, transfer to an oven-proof dish (large enough to make one layer — do not pile enchiladas on top of each other or they will break). Cover with sauce, add the cheese, and place in preheated oven for 10-15 minutes; do not let the sauce dry out. Serve immediately garnished with chopped lettuce, avocado slices, radish rosettes, and a favorite Mexican rice. Stir yogurt and place on the table in a serving dish.

ENCHILADAS SUIZAS (SWISS ENCHILADAS)

2½ cups Swiss cheese, grated   **2 cups plain yogurt**

This variation is prepared in individual oven-proof casseroles with 4 enchiladas to each serving. Add 2 cups plain yogurt to the green tomatillo sauce, add some of the shredded Swiss cheese (in place of the Manchego or Jack cheese) to the shredded chicken, and proceed as above. About 5 minutes before removing from oven, cover with remaining shredded Swiss cheese and return to oven 5 minutes. Serves 6.

PAVO RELLENO DE PICADILLO
(Turkey Stuffed with Minced Meat)

Turkey stuffed with ground beef has now become one of the main dishes when Mexicans celebrate Christmas or New Year's Eve. Luis has created a unique and savory stuffing which has been the delight of our family and friends for such festivities.

2 medium potatoes
¼ cup corn oil
½ lb. ground beef
½ onion
1 cup frozen peas
1 cup black olives, chopped
½ cup pecan pieces

½ cup pine nuts
½ cup raisins
Pepper to taste
½ tsp. salt
2 cups red wine (high quality)
10-lb. young turkey
½ cup salted butter

Preheat oven at 325 degrees F (162 degrees C).

Peel and cut potatoes in small cubes. Heat oil in a heavy skillet over medium heat; sauté the potatoes with the ground beef for 15 minutes. Mince the onion and add to the fried meat; continue simmering for 3 minutes more. Add the peas, olives, pecans, pine nuts, and raisins to the meat; simmer another 5 minutes. Season with pepper and salt (remember the butter is salted). Add 1 cup of wine, stir, and let simmer for 2 minutes.

Remove giblets, liver, and neck from turkey, and discard. Rinse turkey thoroughly under cold running water; pat dry with paper towels. Spread pats of butter in the cavity and add the remaining 1 cup wine into the cavity. Lightly stuff dressing into body cavity of turkey. Tuck legs under flap of skin around tail. Close cavity with skewers and truss. Tie ends of legs to tail with cord. Lift wing tips up and over back, and tuck under bird.

Place turkey on a roasting rack, breast side up. Brush entire bird with vegetable oil. Bake at 325 degrees F (162 degrees C) until turkey browns, about 30 minutes. Then cover with aluminum foil to prevent the turkey from overbrowning (about 2½ to 3 hours). Let turkey stand 15 minutes before carving. Serves 6.

POLLO EN PIPIAN
(Chicken with Pipian Sauce)

Besides corn, squashes and pumpkins were cultivated in ancient Mexico in great variety, mainly for the seeds, which were rich and nutritious and could be stored for times of need. Squash seeds, or *pepitas,* are still available in Mexican markets, roasted and sold like peanuts or shelled and ground to make greenish sauces such as "pipian."

2 (3 lb.) roasting chickens
2 garlic cloves
¼ cup corn oil
15 tomatillos
2 Romaine lettuce leaves
14 sprigs cilantro

½ tsp. cumin
2 serrano chilies
2 cups pepitas (dried green
    pumpkin seeds)
4 cups chicken stock (see index)

Heat oven to 450 degrees F (232 degrees C).

Have your butcher cut the roasting chickens in pieces. Mince garlic; set aside. Rub chicken with oil and minced garlic. Place chickens in oven for 10 minutes. Reduce heat to 350 degrees F (232 degrees C), cover chicken, and continue cooking for 1 hour. Remove chicken from oven and save pan drippings. Turn oven off and return chicken pieces to oven to keep warm until ready to pour sauce.

While the chicken is roasting, make your sauce. Remove husks from tomatillos, and rinse under running water. In a large pot with boiling water, simmer tomatillos until tender. Place tomatillos in blender with rinsed lettuce leaves, rinsed cilantro, cumin, chilies, pepitas, and 1 cup of chicken stock and grind.

Fry the sauce in the pan drippings with the 3 additional cups of chicken stock until the sauce thickens (about 1 hour). Add boiling water if sauce thickens too much. With 10 minutes to go, add the cooked chicken pieces to the sauce. Serves 6.

POLLO EN PIPIAN PREPARADO
(Chicken with Ready-Made Pipian Sauce)

The ready-made pipian paste, "Doña María," is a very popular brand in Mexico, but there are many other brands.

2 (3 lb.) roasting chickens
2 garlic cloves
¼ cup corn oil
10 tomatillos
4 sprigs cilantro

2 serrano chilies
4 cups chicken stock (see index)
1 cup Doña María green pipian
    paste

Heat oven to 450 degrees F (232 degrees C).

Have your butcher cut the roasting chickens in pieces. Mince garlic; set aside. Rub chicken with oil and minced garlic. Place chickens in oven for 10 minutes. Reduce heat to 350 degrees F (176 degrees C), cover chicken, and continue cooking for 1 hour. Remove chicken from oven and save pan drippings. Turn oven off and return chicken pieces to oven to keep warm until ready to pour sauce.

While the chicken is roasting, make your sauce. Remove husks from tomatillos, and rinse under running water. In a large pot with boiling water, simmer tomatillos until tender. Place tomatillos in blender with cilantro, chilies, and 1 cup of chicken stock and grind. Add the green pipian paste to the blender and grind 1 more minute.

Fry the sauce in the pan drippings with the 3 additional cups of chicken stock until sauce thickens (about 1 hour). With 10 minutes to go, add the cooked chicken pieces to the sauce. Serves 6.

CHAPTER 11
BEEF

Native Mexicans before the Spanish conquest did not know about horses or cattle. These animals were brought by the Spaniards when they saw the huge and beautiful grazing lands along the continent from Texas down to the Argentinean Pampas in the South Cone, but the Mexicans did have plenty of deer and they ate plenty of venison. Today, beef is one of the most important staples in the population's diet.

In hot or tropical places, due to the lack of refrigeration, the people have no choice but to dry the meat with salt. This meat is called *cecina* in Mexico and *charqui* in Bolivia and Perú. There are several dishes like the *machaca* which use *cecina* as the main ingredient.

Most of the beef is sold in butcheries all over Mexico, as well as supermarkets in big cities, and it is eaten in the simple and humble tacos as well as steaks and meatballs.

CARNE ASADA A LA TAMPIQUEÑA
(Grilled Beef Tampiqueña Style)

This is one of the most delicious national dishes of Mexico, served in the humblest to the fanciest restaurants. Two days in advance, you can prepare the totopos, refried beans, and rajas with onion. The day before, you can prepare the mole and shredded chicken for the enchiladas and you can even grate the cheese. The day you serve this fabulous dish, all you have to do is marinate and grill your beefsteaks, assemble your enchiladas, and make the guacamole with sliced tomatoes.

1 cup corn oil
4 cloves garlic, minced
1 tsp. oregano leaves
Salt and pepper to taste
6 beefsteaks
1 recipe rajas with onion (see index)
1 recipe refried beans (see index)

1 cup Manchego or Jack cheese, shredded
1 recipe totopos (see Refried Beans)
1 recipe chicken enchiladas with mole sauce (see index)
1 recipe guacamole (see index)
1 tomato, sliced
½ cup plain yogurt, stirred

One or two days in advance, mix the oil with garlic, oregano, and salt and pepper to taste. Four hours before grilling the beefsteaks, marinate them in this oil. Heat grill to 500 degrees F (260 degrees C). Drain beefsteaks and grill about 15 to 20 minutes, turning them frequently.

To serve, place a beefsteak on each plate, then to one side serve the rajas with onion, some refried beans garnished with grated cheese and a totopo, and finally an enchilada and a tablespoon of guacamole. Add tomato slices and dabs of yogurt. Serves 6.

CARNE ASADA
(Grilled Steak)

12 steaks, ¼ inch thick
1 cup corn oil
1½ tsp. oregano
Salt and pepper to taste

2 cups orange juice
½ cup lime juice
4 tsp. red wine vinegar
12 slices of orange, in rounds

On a cutting board, spread the steaks with corn oil and season with oregano, salt, and pepper. Add the orange juice, lime juice, and vinegar and let marinate for 2 hours.

Preheat grill to 500 degrees F (260 degrees C).

Drain marinade from steak and set aside to brush steak as it broils. Transfer steaks to pan under broiler for 6 to 8 minutes turning twice and brush now and then with the marinade.

Garnish with orange slices. Accompany with rajas, avocado slices, rice, and beans. Serves 6.

ROSBIF
(Roast Beef)

2 carrots, whole
6 cloves garlic, whole
5- to 6-lb. roast beef
1 stick butter or margarine (½ cup)
1 bay leaf

1 onion, whole
1 cup beer
6 red potatoes, peeled, whole
Salt to taste

Preheat oven to 500 degrees F (260 degrees C).

Peel carrots. Remove skins from garlic. With a sharp knife make two holes from tip to tip of the beef. Slide one carrot in each hole. With a sharp knife, make 6 small holes on the top of the roast beef. Fill each hole with a whole clove of garlic. Place roast beef in a roasting pan. Cover roast beef with pats of butter. Place beef uncovered in oven to roast for 8-10 minutes. Lower heat to 350 degrees F (176 degrees C) and remove beef from oven. Add bay leaf and whole onion to beef plus beer. Return to oven and let roast for about 1 hour. Add peeled whole potatoes and cook 1 hour longer. Adjust salt. Serves 6.

FILETE MEXICANO
(Mexican Steak)

This beefsteak gets its name from the red, green, and white colors it shares with the Mexican flag. Prepare the steak with the chili sauce and beer and then accompany with the red bell pepper strips, peas, and mashed potatoes. There will be enough chili sauce to use as gravy for the potatoes.

2 ancho chilies	2 fresh red bell peppers
2 serrano chilies	1 white onion
2 tomatoes	3 cups fresh or frozen peas
4 cloves garlic	¼ cup corn oil
6 potatoes	6 beef loin tip steaks, ¼ inch thick
1 stick margarine or butter (½ cup)	2 cups beer
½ cup milk	Salt and pepper to taste

In a saucepan bring some water to boil, turn heat off, and soak ancho chilies in water for 15 minutes, until soft. Discard water and rinse chilies. Remove seeds and stems from chilies. In a blender grind the ancho chilies, serrano chilies, tomatoes, and garlic until a paste is formed. Set aside.

Peel potatoes; cut in quarters. Bring 5 cups water to a boil, transfer potatoes to boiling water, reduce heat, and semi-cover pot. Let simmer for 20-25 minutes, until a fork can easily be inserted in potatoes. Pour water off potatoes. With an electric beater (or potato masher) mash potatoes until all the lumps have disappeared. Now add the butter or margarine and continue beating. Pour the milk in last and beat until fluffy. Place mashed potatoes on an oven-proof earthenware serving dish and keep in warm 150 degree F (65 degree C) oven until ready to serve.

Slice the red bell peppers in strips; set aside. Slice onion on the diagonal; set aside. In a heavy frying pan fry the red bell peppers and onion until golden (10-15 minutes). Transfer these vegetables to an oven-proof earthenware dish in the warm oven until ready to use.

In a small saucepan bring ¾ cup water to a boil, add the peas and 3 pats of butter or margarine, and cook for 15-20 minutes, until peas are tender. Drain all liquid and garnish with a couple extra pats of butter. Place in an oven-proof earthenware dish in warm oven to keep warm.

In a heavy frying pan with hot oil, fry the steaks until browned (about 10-15 minutes). Pour sauce over the steaks and let simmer for 15 minutes more. Add beer (room temperature) and let continue simmering (30 minutes more). Adjust salt and pepper. Serve immediately. Arrange ingredients so that the red bell pepper, green peas, and mashed potatoes make the colors of the Mexican flag and serve the beef in a separate casserole. Serves 6.

MILANESAS
(Beefsteak Milanesa Style)

If you order a *milanesa* on any Mexican menu, this is what they will probably serve you. It is a very popular recipe among housewives also.

½ cup corn oil	12 breakfast steaks
2 eggs, beaten	½ cup Italian bread crumbs

Heat oil in a heavy frying pan. Beat eggs in a mixing bowl. Dip beefsteaks in beaten eggs, then in bread crumbs. Transfer to heated oil and fry for 4 to 5 minutes on each side. Serve immediately. Serves 6.

GUISADO DE CARNE DE RES
(Hearty Mexican Stew)

At least two days every week most homes in Mexico make some version of stew. The most important reason for this phenomenon is that the peas, carrots, potatoes, tomatoes, corn, and many other vegetables are available, it seems, year-round. Secondly, as you know if you have lived in Mexico, the quality, texture, and flavor of these tender fresh vegetables are unequaled.

¼ cup corn oil	6 potatoes
3 lb. beef stew	3 carrots
1 medium white onion	3 ears corn
2 large tomatoes	1 cup peas, fresh or frozen
2 cloves garlic	16 medium mushrooms
1 tsp. whole black peppercorns	1 cup water
6 jalapeño chilies, whole	Salt to taste
1 cup red wine	

In a dutch oven, heat the oil and fry the beef until browned (about 10 minutes), turning frequently to brown all sides.

In a blender, grind the onion, tomatoes, and garlic. Pour this sauce over the meat, add peppercorns and chilies, and bring to a boil. Add wine, reduce heat, and let simmer 10 minutes.

Peel potatoes and cut in halves. Peel carrots and slice. Shuck corn and slice in 2-inch-thick rounds. Clean mushrooms, discard stems, and slice. Add these vegetables to beef mixture and let simmer another 10 minutes. Add 1 cup water and salt to taste and let simmer until vegetables are cooked (about 45 minutes). Serves 6.

TOSTADAS DE CARNE DE RES
(Beef Tostadas)

The secret to a good tostada is to brown the tortilla until crispy and hard enough to hold the refried beans, shredded beef, vegetables, cheese, and sauces. The art is to eat one without making a mess. Tostadas are so delicious that they are eaten everywhere, from the small markets in villages to the fancy fondas in the Zona Rosa of Mexico City. They are simply fun food that private homes of all socio-economic classes can enjoy.

1 recipe refried beans (see index)	12 Romaine lettuce leaves
1 recipe ranch sauce (see index)	½ cup white onion, chopped
6 cloves garlic	1 bunch radishes
3 lb. flank steak	2 cups Manchego or Jack cheese, grated
½ cup corn oil	
1 12-oz. can beer, room temperature	1 cup yogurt
	½ cup corn oil
Salt to taste	24 corn tortillas

Before beginning your tostada recipe, prepare 1 recipe refried beans and 1 recipe of salsa ranchera.

Put garlic through garlic press and spread over beef. Heat covered skillet with ½ cup oil and brown meat uncovered. When brown on all sides, add beer and cook covered about 1 ½ to 2 hours, or until meat is tender. Remove beef from stove and let cool. When beef is cool, shred it and season with salt.

Rinse lettuce leaves, cut in 1-inch pieces, set aside. Slice the radishes. Stir the yogurt to soften and place in an earthenware serving dish for a garnish.

In a heavy frying pan, heat ½ cup oil and fry each tortilla until crispy and hard, turning to brown both sides. Drain on paper towels. Place tortillas in warm 150 degree F (65 degree C) oven.

On each fried tortilla, spread refried beans, a generous helping of shredded beef, the ranch sauce, grated cheese, yogurt, and vegetables. Serves 6.

ENCHILADAS DE CARNE DE RES
(Beef Enchiladas)

These enchiladas have a roasted flavor. While the meat is roasting you can make the sauce. Assembly is done once the meat and sauce are complete. This is an easy recipe. Serve these enchiladas with the lettuce, radishes, and avocados as garnishes in individual serving bowls for everyone to serve himself or herself if they like.

¼ cup corn oil
2 tbsp. red wine vinegar
1 tsp. pequín chili
2 lb. beefsteak (¼ inch thick)
1 recipe roasted ranch sauce (see index)
24 tortillas
1 cup Manchego or Jack cheese, shredded

1 cup plain yogurt
1 head Romaine lettuce
2 Haas avocados
1 bunch radishes
Mesquite chips
Barbecue grill

Mix the oil, vinegar, and pequín chili. Pour over steak and let it marinate for 4 hours in refrigerator.

Next prepare the roasted ranch sauce.

Drain marinade from meat. Grill marinated meat over mesquite charcoal or cook it rapidly under the broiler at 500 degrees F (260 degrees C) about 15 minutes. Slice the steak in thin strips (about 1 inch by ½ inch). Sprinkle the sliced steak with some of the ranch sauce so it will be moist.

Preheat oven to 350 degrees F (177 degrees C).

Heat the tortillas on griddle. Fill with a generous portion of grilled beef and roll closed with the seam side down. Fry them in a heavy frying pan until crispy. Place in an oven-proof casserole in a single layer and cover with remaining roasted ranch sauce. Put this casserole in the preheated oven for 15-20 minutes at 350 degrees F (177 degrees C.). Remove from oven and sprinkle grated cheese and yogurt on top. Return to oven for another 5 minutes.

Clean lettuce and cut in 1-inch pieces. Slice the avocado for garnishing and slice the radishes in rounds. Garnish the enchiladas with the pieces of Romaine lettuce, the avocado slices, and radishes. Serves 6.

ALBÓNDIGAS EN CHIPOTLE
(Meatballs in Chipotle Chili Sauce)

These meatballs *(albóndigas)* are prepared regularly in most Mexican kitchens. This recipe was the one used by Marcelina Peña Vda. de Juarez, to whom this book is dedicated.

4 eggs
4 tomatoes
½ onion
1-2 smoked chipotle chilies (canned)
2 cups beef stock or use granulated
    beef stock
1 lb. ground beef
1 lb. ground pork

½ cup onion, diced
1 tsp. dry mustard
1 tbsp. Worcestershire sauce
¼ tsp. cumin, powdered
1 egg, raw
¼ cup oil
Salt to taste

In a small pan cover 4 eggs with water. Cover pan, bring to a boil, turn heat off, leave on burner, and let sit 15 minutes. Eggs will hard-boil. Remove from heat and run eggs under cold running water. Peel eggs and chop. Set eggs aside for later use.

Roast the tomatoes and ½ onion on a griddle. Place the roasted ingredients in a blender with the chipotle chilies and grind. Pour the ground tomato sauce into a large heavy pot. Bring the sauce to a boil, reduce heat, and add the beef stock. Let simmer 5-10 minutes.

With an electric mixer on stir, mix the beef and pork together with the diced onion, dry mustard, Worcestershire sauce, cumin, and raw egg. Make flat patty shapes and fill with chopped egg. Close each patty into a ball shape. In a heavy frying pan, heat oil over medium heat and fry the meatballs until browned on all sides, being extremely careful not to let the meatballs open. With a slotted spoon, remove the fried meatballs from the frying pan and place them in the tomato sauce. Continue simmering on very low heat for 45 minutes. Turn heat off and let cool. Once cool, remove the grease from the top of the tomato sauce. Adjust salt. Reheat when ready to serve. Serves 6.

CHILES RELLENOS
(Stuffed Poblano Chilies)

You will usually be asked if you want beef- or cheese-stuffed chilies. The following recipe provides for everyone to have two of beef and one of cheese. Poblano chilies are seasonal. We have used California chilies with some success when we tired of waiting for August to come around, but it is best to use the real poblano chilies. Every family has its own "family recipe" for the filling, so feel free to adjust this recipe, which comes from the late Marcelina Peña Vda. de Juarez.

18 poblano chilies
¼ cup corn oil
2 lb. ground beef
¼ onion, chopped
½ cup almonds, peeled and
   chopped
½ cup pine nuts
¼ cup raisins
6 large tomatoes

4 cups chicken stock or use
   granulated chicken stock
10 egg whites
10 egg yolks
½ cup flour
Salt and pepper
1 lb. Manchego or Jack cheese,
   sliced in strips
½ cup corn oil

On two (or three) hot griddles on medium heat, roast all the poblano chilies until black spots appear on their skins. Place the roasted chilies in a cellophane bag until they form vapor (about 10 minutes). Remove one chili at a time and peel raised skin. Try not to let vapor escape from bag. Leaving stem intact, cut one side of each chili (for filling) and remove the seeds. Carefully rinse each chili under running water and dry with paper towels. Set chilies aside on a platter.

Heat ¼ cup oil in a heavy frying pan on medium-high heat and fry beef and onion for 10 minutes. Reduce heat to low and mix in chopped almonds, pine nuts, and raisins. Let simmer 25 minutes covered. Transfer to a mixing bowl for later use.

In a blender, grind tomatoes with cool chicken stock. Transfer to a large soup pot and simmer.

In a 5-quart electric mixer on high speed, stiffly beat egg whites. Add egg yolks and beat for 1 last second just until mixed. Do not overbeat egg yolks with whites or they will get runny.

Mix flour with salt and pepper in a dish with sides.

Fill 12 prepared chilies with beef mixture and 6 chilies with cheese strips. Heat the ½ cup remaining oil on high heat. Dip filled chilies in flour and then in the egg mixture. Deep-fry until chilies are golden brown on all sides. Transfer to oven-proof platter in warm 150 degree F oven (65 degree C) until ready to serve. Heat tomato sauce just before serving and transfer chilies to this sauce. Serve immediately. Serves 6.

EMPANADAS DE CARNE DE RES
(Beef Empanadas)

Several excellent Argentinean restaurants in Mexico City offer beef empanadas on their menu. These empanadas are generally fried. The Mexican people, who already had their own version of masa empanadas filled with cheese or flour empanadas filled with sweet jellies, were eager to try these South American beef empanadas. Here is a recipe for baked empanadas, which many people prefer to the fried ones.

1 lb. sirloin steak	1 tbsp. Worcestershire sauce
2 large red potatoes	Salt and pepper to taste
1½ cups beef stock or dry beef granules	¼ cup black olives (Calamato), sliced
¼ cup onion, minced	⅓ cup raisins
¼ cup corn oil	½ cup peas, frozen
1 tsp. pequín chili, ground	1 cup cold water
½ tsp. cumin, ground	3 envelopes gelatin
1 tsp. dry mustard	2 eggs, hard boiled, chopped

Have your butcher chop your meat in small bite-size pieces. Prepare the filling 4 hours in advance because it needs to gel before filling pastry. (Pastry also needs to be prepared 4 hours in advance.)

Peel and chop potatoes in small cubes; set aside. In a heavy frying pan heat oil, fry beef, potatoes, beef stock, and onion for 10 minutes. Then add chili, cumin, dry mustard, Worcestershire sauce, salt, and pepper and simmer 15 minutes covered. Add olives, raisins and peas to meat. In the cold water, dissolve gelatin. Remove beef mixture from stove and add dissolved gelatin to it. Once cool, transfer to refrigerator for at least 4 hours.

PASTRY

3 cups all-purpose flour	2 tsp. vinegar
1 ½ tsp. salt	2 egg yolks
3 tbsp. sugar	¾ cup ice-cold water
1 cup shortening	

In a 5-quart bowl of an electric mixer, on stir speed, mix the flour, salt, sugar, and shortening until it forms pea shapes, about 4-5 minutes. Mix in the vinegar, the egg yolks, and enough water for dough to form a pliable ball. Mix well, about 2 minutes. Divide dough into 1-inch balls and refrigerate for 4 hours or more if you wish. Remove dough from refrigerator and let stand at room temperature for ½ hour.

Preheat oven to 375 degrees F (191 degrees C). Flatten the balls to saucer shapes, fill each with 1 tablespoon of the gelled beef filling and chopped hard-boiled eggs and fold in half to close; with your thumb and forefinger twist the seam closed. They should have little twists like dinosaurs down the back. Make sure they are sealed or the juice will escape. Bake 10-15 minutes at 425 degrees F (218 degrees C) or until dough is golden. Serves 6.

ESPAGUETI
(Spaghetti with Meat Sauce)

This recipe was given to Luis in the 1960s by an Italian friend living in Mexico City. Mexican people love spaghetti and this cookbook would not be complete without a Mexican version of spaghetti.

1 lb. sirloin beef (½ inch thick)	**¼ tsp. oregano**
5 large tomatoes	**1 tbsp. Worcestershire sauce**
½ onion	**2 bay leaves**
2 cloves garlic	**1 cup good quality red wine**
6 oz. mushrooms	**1 pkg. extra-long spaghetti**
¼ cup corn oil	**1 cup fresh Parmesan cheese,**
1 cup hot water	**grated**

Have your butcher cut your sirloin into bite-size cubes.

Place aluminum foil on a griddle, heat and roast the tomatoes, onion, and garlic. Place the roasted ingredients in a blender and grind; set aside for later use.

Wash, dry, and slice mushrooms; discard stems. Heat oil in a heavy frying pan on medium heat; fry meat until browned. Add mushrooms until they release their juice. Add the roasted tomato sauce and bring sauce to a boil. Reduce heat and add the hot water, oregano, Worcestershire sauce, and bay leaves. When the meat sauce is thickened, add the wine to the sauce and simmer another 30 minutes on very low heat. Turn heat off and set aside until ready to use. Reheat just before serving.

In a large pot ¾ full of water, bring water to boil, add 2 tablespoons oil to water, add spaghetti, and let cook over medium heat for 25 minutes (or according to individual package specifications) until it is well cooked, because Mexicans don't like their spaghetti "al dente." To test for doneness, with a fork, remove one spaghetti and taste. Serve with meat sauce and garnish with cheese. Serves 6.

HAMBURGUESAS CASERAS
(Home-Made Hamburgers)

This is the Mexican version of hamburgers. If you are already a hamburger lover, you are in for a real treat.

3 lb. sirloin steak	6 red potatoes
3 large tomatoes, peeled	1 cup corn oil
3-6 jalapeño chilies	½ white onion
1 white onion	2 eggs
2 tbsp. mustard	2 tbsp. Worcestershire sauce
3 tbsp. red wine vinegar	
1 tsp. each of salt and pepper, or to taste	

Have your butcher remove all fat from sirloin steak and grind it fresh.

With two knives, chop the tomatoes, jalapeños, and 1 onion. With a spoon, stir in the mustard, red wine vinegar, salt, and pepper.

Peel and slice the potatoes into thin round slices. In a heavy frying pan, heat ½ cup oil on medium heat. Fry potato rounds until browned, a batch at a time so they do not crowd (about 10 minutes each batch). Drain each batch on paper towels and place on an oven-proof platter in warm oven until ready to serve.

With two knives, finely chop the ½ onion. In mixing bowl, mix ground meat with onion, eggs, and Worcestershire sauce. Shape into 12 patties.

Heat ½ cup oil in heavy skillet. Fry patties until well done (10-15 minutes), turning three times.

In a serving dish offer sauce to garnish hamburgers. Place hamburgers on a serving platter with fried potato rounds on one side. Serves 6.

CHAPTER 12
PORK

Domestic hogs were not known in Latin America in pre-Columbian times until they were introduced to Mexico by the conquistadors. Wild hogs existed in some parts of the American continent; these were eaten by natives all along the Americas. In Mexico domestic hogs are now raised everywhere, from the humble peasant hut with its pigsty to the big hog ranches where they are raised for commercial purposes.

Pork is one of the favorite ingredients in Mexican cuisine. The famous *carnitas* (literally "the little meats") are sold everywhere you go. There are even special restaurants where only *carnitas* are sold, like The Venadito (the little deer), located in a well-to-do *colonia* (neighborhood) in Mexico City. There are many other typical restaurants that specialize in *carnitas*, like at the entrance of the Mexico City to Cuernavaca highway.

PUERCO EN SALSA DE PIPIAN
(Pork with Pipian Sauce)

6 garlic cloves, whole
2 white onions, whole
4½ lb. boneless pork loin, in
   chunks
6 Romaine lettuce leaves
36 sprigs cilantro
5 to 6 serrano chilies
15 tomatillos

½ tsp. cumin
2½ cups pepitas (dried green
   pumpkin seeds)
¼ cup corn oil
2 cubes Chicken Knorr Swiss
   granules
Salt to taste
9 tbsp. sesame seeds

In a large heavy pot bring 3¾ quarts (15 cups) water to a boil. Add 2 whole cloves garlic and 1 whole onion. Let boil 1 minute, add pork pieces, and reduce heat to medium. Let pork cook uncovered 2 hours, or until pork is tender. Turn heat off and remove pork from liquid. Discard onion and garlic.

Quarter remaining onion. Peel 4 garlic cloves. Rinse lettuce leaves. Remove stems from cilantro and rinse leaves. Place onion, garlic, and lettuce in blender. Chop cilantro and chilies and add to blender. Remove husks from tomatillos, and rinse under running water. In a large pot with boiling water, add tomatillos, reduce heat to medium, and simmer the tomatillos until tender (about 10-15 minutes). Place tomatillos in blender with cumin and all the green pumpkin seeds ("pepitas"). Now grind all blender ingredients with 1 cup water until a smooth sauce is formed.

In a heavy deep pot, sauté the sauce in hot oil. Add the pork pieces and chicken granules and continue to cook until sauce thickens with 3 additional cups of water (about 1 hour). Add 4 tablespoons hot water if sauce gets too thick, and simmer a little longer. Adjust salt and garnish with sesame seeds. Serves 6.

PUERCO EN SALSA DE
PIPIAN YA PREPARADA
(Pork with Ready-Made Pipian Sauce)

Most Mexican cooks use this ready-made pipian paste. "Doña María" is the most popular brand in Mexico, but there are many other brands.

2 garlic cloves
1 whole onion
3 lb. boneless pork loin, in pieces
10 tomatillos
4 sprigs cilantro

2 serrano chilies
4 cups chicken stock (see index)
1 cup pipian paste
¼ cup corn oil

In a large heavy pot bring 6 cups water to a boil. Add garlic and onion. Let boil 1 minute, add pork pieces, reduce heat to medium, and let cook 1 hour, or until pork is tender. Turn heat off and remove pork from stock. Discard onion, garlic and pork stock.

Remove husks from tomatillos, and rinse under running water. In a large pot with boiling water, simmer the tomatillos until tender. Place tomatillos in blender with rinsed cilantro, chilies, 1 cup of chicken stock, and grind. Add the pipian paste to the blender and grind 1 minute more.

In a heavy deep pot, sauté the sauce in the oil. Add the pork pieces with 3 additional cups of chicken stock and continue to cook until sauce thickens (about 1 hour). Add boiling water if sauce gets too thick. Serves 6.

CHULETAS DE PUERCO
(Pork Chops)

¼ cup corn oil
2 tbsp. red wine vinegar

1 tsp. pequín chili
12 pork chops (½ inch thick)

Mix the oil, vinegar, and pequín chili. Pour this over pork chops and let marinate for 4 hours in refrigerator. Drain marinade from meat and set marinade aside for basting. Heat grill to 500 degrees F (260 degrees C). Grill marinated meat over mesquite charcoal or in oven broiler about 45 minutes, turning and basting frequently with marinade. Accompany with a favorite salsa, Mexican rice, and squash. Serves 6.

POZOLE
(Pork and Hominy Stew)

This is a national dish and it is usually made with the pig's head or feet. If you wish to prepare your stew this traditional way feel free to do so; however, here we have given our home recipe for this delicious dish.

2 ancho chilies, ground
1 onion, whole
1 clove garlic, whole
2 bay leaves
1 sprig thyme
2 lb. boneless pork
16 oz. hominy (canned)
Salt to taste

2 cups shredded lettuce
1 whole onion, chopped
6 radishes, sliced
¼ cup oregano leaves
¼ cup pequín chili or cayenne
   pepper, ground
Plenty of lime wedges

Rinse ancho chilies in hot water for 15 minutes, remove stems and seeds, and grind in blender with ¼ cup water.

In a heavy soup pot, bring 10 cups water to a boil and add ground ancho chilies, whole onion, garlic, bay leaves, and thyme. Chop pork in 1-inch pieces and add to boiling water mixture. Let cook on medium heat for 1 hour, reduce heat, add hominy, and let cook 15 to 20 minutes more. Adjust salt.

Place lettuce, chopped onion, radishes, oregano, ground chili, and limes in serving dishes and offer as garnishes for each eater. Serves 6.

TACOS HECHOS DE CARNITAS AL HORNO
(Baked-Pork Tacos)

The authentic *carnitas* ("browned pork") made by most Mexican cooks in time would produce a cardiologist's nightmare — the original cooking method is to use approximately five quarts of pork fat or lard and to deep-fry the pork for two hours until cooked and then crispy. The method below might increase your lifespan a few years by eliminating the deep-frying technique yet it sacrifices nothing in flavor.

4 lb. pork loin or other pork roast
8 cloves garlic, whole
½ cup corn oil
1 white onion, whole
2 bay leaves
½ tsp. rosemary

1 (12 oz.) can beer, room
   temperature
Salt and pepper to taste
24 corn tortillas
1 recipe green tomatillo sauce
   (see index)

With a small sharp knife, pierce pork 8 times and insert a clove of garlic in each pierced spot. Heat oven to 500 degrees F (260 degrees C). Place meat in a covered roasting pan (uncovered). Baste pork with oil. Place under oven broiler until it browns on top, bottom, and sides. Remove browned pork from oven and reduce temperature to 300 degrees F (148 degrees C). Place whole onion on side of meat. Add bay leaves, rosemary, and beer. Adjust salt and pepper. Cover, return to oven, and bake 2 hours, or until pork is well done.

Heat griddle to warm tortillas. With a sharp knife, carve meat into 1½-inch pieces. Heat the tortillas on the griddle and place in a napkin-lined basket. Serve the pork on a serving platter. Each person can fill and roll his own tortilla. Offer green tomatillo salsa on the side.

TACOS HECHOS DE CARNITAS HERVIDAS
(Boiled-Pork Tacos)

There is no need to add any oil to this recipe. As the pork boils in the water, the pork fat is released, the water is absorbed, and the pork is browned the last few minutes. It is truly delicious rolled inside a tortilla.

1 tsp. oregano
1 tsp. cumin
1 whole onion
4 lb. pork shoulder

Salt to taste
24 corn tortillas
1 recipe roasted green tomatillo
   sauce (see index)

Fill a 5-quart heavy pot with water and bring to a boil. Add oregano, cumin, and whole onion; let boil 3 minutes. Add pork and salt to taste, let boil 1 minute more, reduce heat, cover, and simmer 2½ hours, or until water is consumed. Brown pork in its own juices (about 10 minutes). Pour off any excess fat.

Heat griddle to warm tortillas. With a sharp knife, carve meat into 1½-inch pieces. Heat the tortillas on the griddle and place in a napkin-lined basket. Serve the pork on a serving platter. Each person can fill and roll his own tortilla. Offer roasted green tomatillo salsa on the side. Serves 6.

CHAPTER 13
FISH

Mexico is one of the few countries with shores on the Pacific and Atlantic oceans and the Caribbean Sea, and it is located on longitudes well known for an abundance of all kinds of fish due to the sea currents. Paradoxically, fish is expensive due to certain political considerations of the so-called fishing unions, which will not let anyone fish unless he belongs to the union. These unions set up prices which are higher than they should be. But in some parts of the Pacific coast you can eat fish and shrimp fried in garlic at a relatively cheap price.

The most common and favored are the *huachinango* (red snapper) and *róbalo* (sea bass). In Mexico City there is a long street with *ostionerias* (seafood restaurants) where you can eat or buy your favorite seafood. You can also buy fish at your supermarket at a slightly high price. Most of the menus in restaurants have one kind or another of a seafood dish, and *huachinango a la veracruzana* would, for sure, be one listed on the menu.

When you buy whole fish, make sure you are getting the freshest by checking that the gills are pink and there is no unpleasant odor.

HUACHINANGO A LA VERACRUZANA
(Red Snapper Veracruz Style)

Red snapper *(huachinango)* is found in the Gulf of Mexico and is quite different from the snapper from the West Coast, which is more oily and less meaty. The red snapper is two to three feet long and weighs up to thirty pounds. Red snappers weighing around three to four pounds are sold whole. The larger fish are cut into fillets. Other species of smaller snapper are sold locally. Mexico has an abundance of the larger and tastier red snappers.

6 large tomatoes, not peeled	Salt to taste
3 to 6 serrano chilies	1 large red snapper (4 to 5 lb.) or
¼ medium onion	any firm white whole fish
2 cloves garlic	¼ cup olive oil
¼ cup water	6 cloves garlic, minced
½ tsp. oregano leaves	4 tsp. lime juice
1 tsp. dry thyme, ground	6 red potatoes
2 tbsp. corn oil	1 white onion, sliced in rounds
1 cup pimento-stuffed olives, whole	12 lime wedges
2 bay leaves	12 pickled jalapeño chilies

Roast the tomatoes, chilies, ¼ onion, and 2 garlic cloves on hot griddle until they blister. Be careful not to burn. In a blender, grind the roasted ingredients with the water, being careful not to overblend. Add oregano and thyme to sauce in blender and turn on and off about three times. Heat corn oil in heavy frying pan and add tomato sauce, whole olives, and whole bay leaves. Simmer for 2-3 minutes; adjust salt; set aside.

Prepare the fish for baking: rub the inside with olive oil, minced garlic, and lime juice. Lay the fish on a flat surface and measure the highest thickness of the snapper. This measurement is needed to calculate 10 minutes baking time per inch thickness. Place in refrigerator for 20 minutes.

Preheat oven to 325 degrees F (162 degrees C).

Peel and quarter potatoes. Remove fish from refrigerator and drain the marinade from the fish. Place fish in a roasting pan without a wire rack (so the fish will be smothered in the tomato sauce). Place potatoes around fish. Pour tomato sauce over fish, cover with aluminum foil, and place in oven (about 45 minutes to 1 hour).

While the fish is baking, slice onion rounds and lime wedges. Transfer the fish carefully from the roasting pan onto an earthenware-type serving platter. Garnish with the fresh onion slices, jalapeño chilies, and offer lime wedges on a separate serving dish. Serves 6.

ADOBO DE PESCADO
(Fish in Adobo Sauce)

4 ancho chilies
2 juicy oranges
2 tomatoes
1 onion
12 cloves garlic
½ tsp. cumin
¼ tsp. oregano
3 lb. red snapper fillets (about 2 per serving)

¼ cup corn oil
1 bunch radishes
1 head Romaine lettuce
1 cruet for oil
Light olive oil
1 cruet for vinegar
Red wine vinegar

Preheat oven to 375 degrees F (191 degrees C).

In a medium saucepan, boil water, turn heat off, and soak ancho chilies (10 minutes). Remove from hot water and discard stems and seeds. Discard the water. From oranges, squeeze 2 cups juice. In a blender, grind ancho chilies with orange juice; set chili sauce aside.

On a griddle over medium heat, roast the tomatoes, onion, and 6 cloves garlic. Place roasted ingredients in the blender and chop (do not grind). Place this chopped sauce in a saucepan over medium heat, season with cumin and oregano, and simmer for 10 minutes. Add the chili sauce to the tomato sauce and continue to simmer another 5 minutes. Set aside at room temperature until ready to use.

Put remaining 6 cloves garlic through a garlic press. Spread fish fillets with oil and pressed garlic. In an oven-proof earthenware casserole, place a row of fish fillets and smother with the sauce. Place casserole in hot oven and bake, allowing 10 minutes per inch of thickness (approximately 15-20 minutes).

While it is cooking, clean and cut the radishes in florets and cut lettuce into 1-inch pieces for garnishing the fish dish. Place a one-bottle cruet with oil and another with red wine vinegar on the table for each person to season lettuce. Serves 6.

FILETES DE HUACHINANGO
(Red Snapper Fillets)

6 large tomatoes
1 large white onion
3 lb. red snapper fillets (about 2 per serving)
4 tsp. lime juice
¼ cup corn oil
3 cloves garlic, minced

½ tsp. thyme, ground
2 bay leaves
1 cup pimento-stuffed olives, whole
6 jalapeño chilies, whole
Salt to taste
6 limes cut in wedges

Slice the tomatoes into wedges; set aside. Slice onion in rounds; set aside. Rinse fish fillets under cold running water and pat dry with paper towel. Squeeze some lime juice over fillets. In a heavy frying pan, heat oil and sauté garlic 1 minute. Discard garlic, increase heat, and fry fish fillets, calculating 10 minutes for each inch of thickness. Brown one side, turn, and brown other side. Remove fried fish to platter. Now sauté the tomatoes with the onion for 5 minutes. Add the thyme, bay leaves, olives, and whole jalapeño chilies; simmer for 5 minutes more. Now return fish fillets to tomato sauce and let simmer for 1 minute on low heat. Adjust salt. Serve immediately. Offer lime wedges as a garnish. Serves 6.

PESCADO AL MESQUITE
(Fish in Mesquite)

¼ cup corn oil
2 tbsp. red wine vinegar
1 tsp. pequín chili
3 lb. red snapper fillets (about 2 per serving)
1 recipe roasted ranch sauce (see index)

1 head Romaine lettuce
2 Haas avocados
1 bunch radishes
Mesquite charcoal chips
Hinged grill (so the fish will stay in place)

Mix the oil, vinegar, and pequín chili. Pour this over fish fillets and let marinate for 1 hour in refrigerator.

Drain marinade from fish and save for brushing fish. Make sure grill is well oiled when you put the fish into it — so it will mark the fish. Grill marinated fish over hot mesquite charcoal, allowing 10 minutes for each inch of thickness. Brush fish with marinade as it cooks. It needs to be kept well oiled.

Prepare roasted ranch sauce. Clean lettuce and cut in 1-inch pieces. Slice the avocado for garnishing and slice the radishes in rounds. Garnish fish with the pieces of lettuce, the avocado slices, and the radishes. Accompany with roasted ranch sauce. Serves 6.

TRUCHA RELLENA DE PAPA PURÉ
(Trout Stuffed with Mashed Potato)

This dish is delicious.

6 large red potatoes
8 cups water
1 stick butter or margarine (½ cup)
¼ cup milk
1 tsp. fennel seed
½ tsp. pequín chili
Salt and pepper to taste
6 good-sized trout (about 8-12
   inches)

12 cloves garlic
½ cup corn oil
2 bunches radish
3 tomatoes
2 avocados
3 limes

Preheat oven to 450 degrees F (232 degrees C).

Peel potatoes and cut in quarters. Bring water to a boil and transfer potatoes to boiling water. Reduce heat and semi-cover pot; let simmer for 20-25 minutes, until a fork can easily be inserted in potatoes. Pour water off potatoes. With an electric beater (or potato masher) mash potatoes until all the lumps have disappeared. Now add the butter and continue beating. Pour milk in last and beat until fluffy. At this point, add the fennel seed, pequín chili, salt, and pepper. Set aside for stuffing fish.

Clean the fish and prepare for stuffing, leaving the heads intact. Mince the garlic and mix with oil. Rub the inside of fish with ½ of this mixture and some lime juice. Lay the fish on a flat surface and measure the highest thickness of the trout. This measurement is needed to calculate 10 minutes baking time per inch thickness. Place in refrigerator for 20 minutes.

Remove fish from refrigerator. Stuff each trout with the mashed potato filling. Rub remaining garlic-oil mixture over each fish, cover with aluminum foil, and place in preheated oven for approximately 30-45 minutes (allowing 10 minutes per inch of thickness). Carefully remove the trout from the roasting pan with two heavy-duty spatulas and place on a large earthenware platter with garnish below.

Clean radishes and prepare florets. Cut tomato into wedges, and slice avocado. Cut limes in wedges. Arrange these garnishes around fish. Serves 6.

FILETES DE RÓBALO
(Sea Bass Fillets)

Sea bass is a very common fish along the eastern coast of Mexico and is very popular, so we wanted to include a recipe of this fish for you.

2 red bell peppers	**1 medium onion, sliced**
¼ cup red wine vinegar	**2 bay leaves**
1 tsp. salt	**¼ cup chopped parsley**
2 lb. sea bass fillets	**1 tsp. grated nutmeg**
6 medium tomatoes, sliced	**½ cup corn oil**

Preheat oven to 350 degrees F (176 degrees C).

Cut red bell peppers in strips and place them in a glass dish; pour in the vinegar. Sprinkle peppers with salt. Let stand 20 minutes. Discard vinegar.

Rinse fish well, and dry with paper towels. Arrange fish in an oven-proof earthenware casserole, large enough to accommodate all the pieces in no more than two layers. Top each layer of fillets with red bell peppers, as well as the tomato and onion slices, bay leaves, parsley, and nutmeg. Sprinkle with corn oil. Bake until fish flakes easily when tested with a fork. (Allow 10 minutes per inch of thickness.) Serves 6.

PESCADO AL MOJO DE AJO
(Garlic-Smothered Fish)

When referring to white fish, sole probably comes to mind. More frequently, however, white fish is any of the many members of the flounder family.

¼ cup parsley, chopped	**¼ cup corn oil**
12 cloves garlic	**Salt and pepper**
3 pounds fresh fish fillets, (white meat)	**12 jalapeño chilies, pickled**

Mince 6 cloves garlic; set aside. Rinse fish fillets under running water. Dry on paper towels. Spread fish fillets with the minced garlic.

Heat oil in heavy frying pan and sauté 6 whole garlics 1 minute over medium heat; discard these garlics. Add fish fillets to hot oil and fry until fillets are browned.

Remove fillets from frying pan to an earthenware serving platter and garnish with salt and pepper, as well as chopped parsley and whole pickled jalapeños. Serves 6.

EMPANADAS DE CAMARÓN
(Shrimp Empanadas)

1 recipe empanada pastry (see Beef
  Empanadas)
2 cloves garlic
½ white onion
2 jalapeño chilies
2 large tomatoes
¼ cup corn oil

1 cup pimento-stuffed olives,
  chopped
1 lb. medium shrimp
2 pkg. gelatin
1 cup cold water
Salt to taste

First, prepare pastry recipe.

In a blender, mince garlic, onion, and chilies with tomatoes; set aside. Heat oil in a heavy frying pan and sauté sauce 5-10 minutes. Add chopped olives.

Shell shrimp — just push the shell with your thumb and forefinger and it will come off. Remove tail. With a sharp knife cut along the curve in the body and remove the back vein. Chop shrimp, add to sauce mixture, and sauté for 3 to 5 minutes, or until shrimp are cooked (they will turn pink). Do not overcook or the shrimp will become rubbery.

Dissolve gelatin in the cold water. Transfer the dissolved gelatin to the tomato-shrimp mixture. Adjust salt and place mixture in refrigerator for 4 hours or until shrimp gel.

The shrimp empanadas are shaped, closed, and baked exactly like the beef empanadas. Serves 6.

CAMARÓN AL AJILLO-PASILLA
(Shrimp with Garlic and Pasilla)

The shrimp in this recipe is served with rings of pasilla chilies. It is different from the Shrimp in pasilla Sauce. We tasted this recipe a few years ago in a restaurant along Insurgentes Avenue in Mexico City. It was served piping hot in individual metal casserole dishes on top of individual wooden trays with hot crusty bread.

6 pasilla chilies	**36 large fresh shrimp**
2 white onions	**1 tsp. red wine vinegar**
¼ cup olive oil	**6 cloves garlic**

Heat oven to 250 degrees F (120 degrees C).

In a medium saucepan bring 4 cups water to a boil. Turn heat off and place chilies in the hot water to soften, about 10 minutes. Remove chilies from water, drain on paper towels, and discard water. Remove stems and seeds from chilies. Now cut the chilies in 1-inch rounds. Set rounds aside for frying later.

Slice onion in rounds; set aside. In a large heavy frying pan, heat oil and fry onion rings with chili rounds, about 8 minutes. Transfer the fried chilies and onions to an oven-proof earthenware dish and place in oven to keep warm. Reserve oil in frying pan for frying shrimp later.

Shell shrimp — just push the shell with your thumb and forefinger and it will come off. Leave tail intact. With a sharp knife cut along the curve in the body and remove the back vein. Rinse shrimp under cool water. Transfer shrimp to a mixing bowl filled with ice-cold water and the teaspoon of red wine vinegar and place in the refrigerator for 10 minutes.

Mince garlic. Heat oil used to fry onion and chilies, add the minced garlic, and sauté on low heat for 1 minute only. Add the drained shrimp and sauté the shrimp on both sides until pink and cooked (about 3-5 minutes). Transfer the onion rings and chili rounds to sautéed shrimp. Place 6 large shrimp, some onion rings and chili rounds in each of 6 individual oven-proof casseroles and place in the warm oven 5-10 minutes before serving. Serve hot shrimp directly from oven in the individual casseroles. Serves 6.

CAMARONES EN SALSA DE PASILLA
(Shrimp in Pasilla Sauce)

This shrimp recipe is different from the Shrimp with Garlic and Pasilla. The shrimp in this recipe are served on top of a pasilla sauce.

2 pasilla chilies
2 cloves garlic
¼ white onion
1 tomato
36 large fresh shrimp
1 tsp. red wine vinegar

6 cloves garlic
¼ cup olive oil
12 pickled jalapeño chilies (2 for each, if desired)
1 white onion, sliced in rings
2 loaves French bread

In a medium saucepan bring 4 cups water to a boil. Turn heat off and place pasilla chilies in the hot water to soften, about 10 minutes. Remove chilies from water, drain on paper towels, and discard water. Remove stems and seeds from chilies. Place the cleaned chilies in the blender to grind with the 2 cloves garlic, ¼ white onion, and tomato. In a heavy medium pot, saute the sauce until it thickens (about 10 minutes). Set aside at room temperature in an earthenware sauce dish until ready to use.

Shell shrimp — just push the shell with your thumb and forefinger and it will come off; leave tail intact. With a sharp knife cut along the curve in the body and remove the back vein. Rinse shrimp under cool water. Transfer shrimp to a mixing bowl filled with ice-cold water and the teaspoon of red wine vinegar and place in the refrigerator for 10 minutes.

Mince 6 cloves garlic; set aside. Remove shrimp from refrigerator and discard water. Drain chilled shrimp on paper towels. Heat olive oil in a heavy frying pan and sauté the minced garlic on low heat (approximately 1 minute), add the drained shrimp, and sauté the shrimp on both sides until pink and cooked (about 3-5 minutes). Do not overcook shrimp or they will become rubbery. Serve in individual earthenware casseroles, first placing the pasilla sauce on each casserole and on top of the sauce placing 6 shrimp each. Garnish with the 2 pickled jalapeños each and fresh onion rings. Accompany with crusty French bread. Serves 6.

CAMARONES A LA PARRILLA EN MANTEQUILLA POBLANA
(Grilled Shrimp with Poblano Butter)

3 poblano (or California) chilies
1 cup butter or margarine (16 tbsp.)
¼ cup cilantro, chopped

3 cloves garlic, minced
Salt and pepper to taste
36 jumbo shrimp

On a griddle roast the poblano or California chilies until the skins blister. Place these chilies in a cellophane bag and let sweat for 10 minutes. Remove from bag and peel skins as best you can. Remove stem and seeds from each chili and dice. Soften butter and combine with cilantro, garlic, salt, and pepper. Heat grill. Grill shrimp basting with poblano butter. When done, spread lightly with more butter and serve. Serves 6.

ENCHILADAS DE JAIBA
(Crab Meat Enchiladas)

1 recipe green tomatillo sauce (see index)
2 cloves garlic
1 tsp. lime juice
4 tbsp. corn oil
1½ lb. crab meat
1 cup Manchego or Jack cheese, grated

24 corn tortillas
¼ cup corn oil
1 head Romaine lettuce
2 avocados, sliced
12 radishes
½ cup plain yogurt

Prepare green tomatillo sauce before making enchiladas.

Mince garlic. Heat 4 tablespoons oil in a heavy frying pan and sauté flaked crab meat with garlic for 10 minutes. Add lime juice and sauté 1 minute more. Remove from stove and place crab meat in a mixing bowl.

Preheat oven to 350 degrees F (176 degrees C).

Warm tortillas on a hot griddle; place them in a napkin to keep warm. Heat ¼ cup oil in a heavy frying pan and fry the tortillas on both sides until pliable. Remove tortillas from oil and drain on paper towels. Fill each fried tortilla with 3 tablespoons crab meat, 1 teaspoon grated cheese, and some salsa. Roll each tortilla closed, place seam side down in a casserole, cover with remaining salsa, and transfer to the heated oven for 15 to 20 minutes.

Serve garnished with chopped lettuce, avocado slices, radish rosettes, and a favorite Mexican rice. With a fork, stir yogurt and place in a small serving dish to serve as a garnish at the table. Serves 6.

TACOS DE JAIBA
(Crab Meat Tacos)

1 recipe green tomatillo sauce (see index)
¼ cup corn oil
4 tbsp. butter or margarine
¼ cup white onion, chopped
4 cloves garlic, minced
2 canned jalapeño chilies, chopped

2 tbsp. chili juice, from can
1 tomato, peeled, chopped
6 tbsp. fresh cilantro, chopped
Salt and pepper to taste
3 cups crab meat, cleaned
24 corn tortillas

First prepare sauce, then proceed with the recipe for tacos.

Heat oil and butter over low heat in heavy frying pan. Add onion and sauté 3-4 minutes. Add minced garlic and sauté 2-3 minutes more. Add chopped jalapeños, jalapeño chili juice, chopped tomatoes, and chopped cilantro. Season with salt and pepper to taste. Simmer for about 30 minutes. Add shredded crab and simmer another 20 minutes, or until the filling becomes flaky.

Heat tortillas and fill with crab mixture; secure with a toothpick. Serve immediately. Makes 24 tacos.

JAIBAS RELLENAS
(Stuffed Crabs)

2 large tomatoes	3 cloves garlic
½ small onion	¼ cup corn oil
½ cup almonds	1½ lb. crab meat
2 sprigs parsley	12 shell-shaped dishes (or clean crab shells)
6 pimento-stuffed olives, sliced in rounds	1 head Romaine lettuce
½ cup green olives, chopped	1 bunch radishes
¼ cup pine nuts, in pieces	2 fresh tomatoes
2 red bell peppers, sliced	3 limes

Preheat oven to 450 degrees F (232 degrees C).

In a small saucepan bring some water to a boil. Immerse 2 tomatoes briefly, remove, peel skins, and discard water. Cut tomatoes in pieces, place in blender with onion and almonds, and grind. Clean parsley, remove leaves from stems, and add leaves to the blender, turning on for 30 seconds only. Set sauce aside.

Mince the garlic; set aside. In a heavy frying pan, heat oil and sauté bell pepper strips for 10 minutes. Remove from frying pan and set aside on a platter with paper towels to drain. In the same frying pan sauté the minced garlic for 1 minute, add crab meat, and sauté it for 10 minutes. Add the sauce and let simmer 15 minutes. Add the ½ cup chopped olives and pine nuts and continue cooking over low heat for 10 minutes, or until crab mixture dries a little. Place a generous portion of this crab mixture in 12 shell-shaped dishes. Place the crab dishes on a cookie sheet and put in hot oven for 10 minutes, until browned. Garnish each crab dish with two olive rounds (like crab eyes) and 2 bell pepper strips.

Rinse and drain lettuce and cut in 1-inch pieces, set aside. Prepare radishes in florets. Slice 2 unpeeled tomatoes in wedges. Cut limes in wedges. On each of 6 individual serving plates, place 2 crab dishes for each person, garnished with the lettuce, radishes, and tomato and lime wedges. Serves 6.

CHAPTER 14
SALADS

Traditionally, salads are not the pièce de résistance in Mexican cuisine. Mexicans like to garnish tortilla dishes with lettuce, radish, tomato, and avocado, like for enchiladas or tostadas. But following the trend of other countries, contemporary Mexico nowadays cooks up salads for its cosmopolitan population in homes as well as restaurants. There are also vegetarian restaurants where all kinds of salads are served.

Salads in Mexico differ from salads served in the U.S. or Europe. Most of the ingredients, such as potatoes, carrots, and mushrooms, are cooked, not served raw. At dinner, the first course would be a salad with a variety of ingredients dressed with oil and red wine vinegar.

JITOMATES RELLENOS DE LEGUMBRES
(Vegetable-Stuffed Tomatoes)

1 head Romaine lettuce
18 radishes
6 large tomatoes

3 potatoes
1 cup peas, fresh or frozen (not
    canned)

Rinse and dry lettuce on paper towels. Rinse and dry radishes and shape into florets. Cut tomatoes into decorative containers by cutting zigzags across the center of the tomato. Separate the top of each tomato from the bottom, and discard the seedy center.

Bring water to a boil in a medium pot. Peel and quarter the potatoes. Add potatoes to boiling water, reduce heat, and let simmer for 15 minutes, or until potatoes are tender when fork is inserted. Drain water and transfer cooked potatoes to a mixing bowl. Dice potatoes into small cubes.

In a medium pot bring 1 cup water to a boil. Add peas to boiling water. Reduce heat and simmer for about 8-10 minutes, until tender. If using frozen peas, follow directions for cooking on package. Drain water from the peas, and transfer peas to mixing bowl with diced potatoes. Let the potatoes and the peas cool before stuffing the tomatoes.

On individual serving plates arrange 2-3 lettuce leaves and place on top one hollowed-out tomato for each serving. Fill tomatoes with vegetable mixture. Decorate with 3 radishes each. Cover each tomato with a tablespoon of the mayonnaise and serve. Serves 6.

HOMEMADE MAYONNAISE

2 cups corn oil
2 egg yolks
½ tsp. dry mustard

1 tsp. salt
2 tsp. lime juice

Chill a 5-quart mixing bowl, the whisk, and the bottle of oil in the refrigerator at least 1 hour. Beat the egg yolks in the chilled bowl with the whisk. Add mustard and salt and gradually add the chilled oil in a very thin steady stream, beating constantly until well thickened and stiff. Thin with the lime juice to taste. Transfer to a small serving dish and refrigerate.

ENSALADA DE LEGUMBRES
(Vegetable Salad)

1 head Romaine lettuce	2 cups Jack cheese, cut in cubes
2 red potatoes	Salt and pepper to taste
2 eggs	Light olive oil
1 cup frozen white corn kernels	Red wine vinegar
1 cup frozen peas	

Rinse lettuce. Peel potatoes, cut in half, cover with water, and cook over high heat until they come to a boil. Reduce heat and continue to cook on low for 20-25 minutes, until potatoes are well cooked and tender when a fork is inserted. Boil eggs to hard-boiled stage (10 minutes); run cool water over hot eggs to facilitate peeling shells. Cook the corn and peas according to instructions on package. Chop hard-boiled eggs into medium pieces. Place 4 whole lettuce leaves on each plate. Mix the diced potatoes, corn, peas, cheese, and egg. Adjust salt and pepper. Have a cruet on hand with the olive oil and the vinegar for each person to garnish as desired. Serves 6.

ENSALADA DE EJOTES
(String Bean Salad)

3 cups fresh string beans	1 tomato
2 cups water	¼ cup onion, chopped
2 eggs	Oil and red vinegar

Remove the strings from the string beans and cut off the tips. Cut the string beans in 1½-inch julienne slices by first cutting string beans into equal lengths, then cutting them into match-stick strips, i.e., ////. In a large saucepan bring the water to a boil, place string beans in pan, reduce heat, and simmer for 15-20 minutes. Drain water and let string beans cool.

Hard-boil eggs and chop. Dice tomato. In a mixing bowl combine tomato, chopped onion, and string beans. Decorate with chopped eggs. Have on hand a cruet for oil and vinegar to season. Serves 6.

ENSALADA RANCHERA
(Farmer's Salad)

1 head Romaine lettuce	**3 tomatoes**
3 raw carrots	**10 radishes**
3 red potatoes	**1 cucumber**
1 cup peas, fresh or frozen	**Corn oil**
3 eggs	**Red wine vinegar**
½ lb. favorite white cheese	

Rinse the lettuce and cut into thin strips. Peel carrots and grate. Peel potatoes and cut into quarters. In a medium pot bring water to a boil. Add potatoes to boiling water, reduce heat, and let simmer for 15 minutes, until tender when fork is inserted. Drain water and dice potatoes.

In a medium pot bring 1 cup water to a boil, add peas, reduce heat, and let simmer for 8-10 minutes, until peas are tender. If using frozen peas, follow directions on package. Drain water and add peas to the diced potatoes.

Hard-boil eggs and slice. Dice the cheese into ½-inch pieces.

Cut tomatoes into wedges. Slice the radishes into rounds. Dice the cucumber. Mix the lettuce, grated carrots, potatoes, peas, cheese, tomatoes, and cucumber. Decorate with egg slices. Have on hand a cruet for oil and vinegar to season. Serves 6.

ENSALADA DE COLIFLOR
(Cauliflower Salad)

1 large cauliflower	**2 large tomatoes**
3 carrots	**Oil and red vinegar**

Rinse cauliflower and remove outer leaves. In a large saucepan bring 2 cups water to a boil, place cauliflower in pan, reduce heat, and simmer for 15-20 minutes. Drain water and let cauliflower cool. With a knife, slice cauliflower into individual florets.

In a medium pot bring 3 cups water to a boil. Peel carrots, cut them in julienne slices, and drop them in boiling water. Reduce heat and simmer for 15-20 minutes until tender. Drain water and let carrots cool.

With a sharp knife, slice tomatoes in wedges. In a serving bowl, combine the cauliflower, carrots, and tomatoes.

Have on hand a cruet for oil and vinegar to season. Serves 6.

ENSALADA DE PEPINOS
(Cucumber Salad)

1 cup yogurt	Salt and pepper to taste
4 tbsp. onion, minced	4 cucumbers
4 tbsp. red wine vinegar	1 head Romaine lettuce
4 tbsp. cilantro, finely minced	1 bunch radishes

In a mixing bowl, combine the yogurt, onion, vinegar, cilantro, salt, and pepper. Peel the cucumbers and with a fork mark lines down all the sides of the cucumbers (so cucumbers will look decorative when sliced into rounds). Slice cucumbers in rounds. Toss the cucumbers in the yogurt and let stand for 15 minutes.

Rinse lettuce and dry on paper towels. Rinse radishes and cut in florets. Place lettuce leaves on individual salad dishes, top with cucumbers, and decorate with radishes. Serves 6.

AGUACATE RELLENO DE JAIBA
(Crab-Stuffed Avocado)

2 cloves garlic	3 avocados
1 tsp. lime juice	1 head Romaine lettuce
4 tbsp. corn oil	12 radishes
1½ lb. crab meat	12 lime wedges

Mince garlic; set aside. Now in a heavy frying pan, heat oil and sauté flaked crab meat with garlic for 5 minutes. Add lime juice and sauté 1 minute more. Remove from stove and place crab meat in a mixing bowl.

Cut the avocados in half; discard the pits. Squeeze some lime into each avocado half. On individual salad plates place 2 Romaine lettuce leaves. Place the halved avocados on top of the leaves. Fill the avocado halves with the crab meat. On the side of the avocado decorate with radish florets and lime wedges. Serves 6.

AGUACATE RELLENO DE CAMARÓN
(Shrimp-Stuffed Avocado)

1½ lb. medium shrimp
4 qt. water
1 tsp. salt
3 cloves garlic
Lime juice

3 Haas avocados
12 Romaine lettuce leaves
12 radishes, cut in florets
12 limes, cut in wedges

Shell and devein the shrimp. In a large saucepan, bring the water (with the salt) to a boil. Mince garlic and add to the boiling water. Add shrimp to boiling water, reduce heat, and simmer the shrimp for 5 minutes. Discard water, place shrimp in a mixing bowl, and let cool. Squeeze lime juice over the shrimp.

Cut the avocados in half; discard the pit. Squeeze some lime into each avocado half. On individual salad plates place 2 Romaine lettuce leaves. Place the halved avocados on top of the leaves. Fill with the shrimp. On the side of the avocado decorate with radish florets and lime wedges. Serves 6.

AGUACATE RELLENO DE ATÚN
(Tuna-Stuffed Avocado)

1 recipe homemade mayonnaise
   (see Vegetable-Stuffed
   Tomatoes)
3 serrano chilies
1 white onion
1 (6½ oz.) can white tuna chunks

3 Haas avocados
Lime juice
12 Romaine lettuce leaves
12 radishes, cut in florets
12 limes, cut in wedges

First prepare mayonnaise.

Chop chilies and onion. Drain oil from tuna fish; add the onion and chilies. Add 4 tablespoons of the homemade mayonnaise to the tuna fish and mix well.

Cut the avocados in half; discard the pit. Squeeze some lime into each avocado half. On individual salad plates place 2 Romaine lettuce leaves. Place the halved avocados on top of the leaves. Fill with the tuna fish. On the side of the avocado decorate with radish florets and lime wedges. Serves 6.

ENSALADA DE CAMARONES
(Shrimp Salad)

1 recipe homemade mayonnaise (see Vegetable-Stuffed Tomatoes)	2 cucumbers
	1 red bell pepper
36 medium fresh shrimp	1 head Romaine lettuce
1 tsp. red wine vinegar	12 green onions, whole
2 potatoes	36 black olives, whole
3 eggs	¼ cup cilantro, minced
	6 limes, cut in wedges

First prepare the mayonnaise.

Shell shrimp — just push the shell with your thumb and forefinger and it will come off; remove tail. With a sharp knife cut along the curve in the body and remove the back vein. Rinse shrimp under cool water. Transfer shrimp to a mixing bowl filled with ice-cold water and then add the red wine vinegar. Place in the refrigerator for 10 minutes.

Remove shrimp from refrigerator and discard water. Dry shrimp on paper towels. Sauté shrimp for 3 to 5 minutes, or until shrimp are cooked (they will turn pink). Do not overcook or the shrimp will become rubbery.

In a medium pot, bring 5 cups water to a boil. Peel and quarter potatoes, drop into boiling water, reduce heat, and simmer for 15-20 minutes, until tender when a fork is inserted.

In a small pot, hard-boil eggs. Slice into rounds.

Peel cucumbers. With a fork mark lines down all the sides of the cucumbers (so that they will be more decorative when sliced). Slice the cucumbers in rounds. Discard top and seeds of red bell pepper; slice into thin strips.

Rinse and dry lettuce. Cut ends of green onions off and rinse and dry onions.

In a mixing bowl, combine potatoes and 4 tablespoons of homemade mayonnaise.

This salad is set in a wooden salad bowl lined with lettuce, potato salad in the center with the shrimp set upright around the potato salad, and an alternating decoration of the sliced boiled egg, green onions, cucumbers, black olives, and bell pepper strips. Finally, sprinkle the chopped cilantro over the potato salad. Offer lime wedges for garnish. Serves 6.

CHAPTER 15
VEGETABLES

The abundance of vegetables in Mexico is unique, due to the various climates to be found in its high mountains, valleys, mesas, and tropical lands. Most of the vegetables are not seasonal, but grow year round. Peas in their pods are to be found in any *mercado* (open market) or supermarket all year round and at excellent prices. Potatoes and tomatoes have a rich flavor, since they are grown in most cases without pesticides. Lettuce also has a rich and fresh flavor. Without being nationalist or patriotic we can say that vegetables produced in Mexico are some of the best in the world. Vegetables are served as side dishes, in salads, and in soups.

CALABACITAS
(Zucchini Squash)

6 zucchini squash
¼ onion
1 tomato
3 strips bacon

2 tbsp. corn oil
1 tsp. chicken bouillon (preferably
   Knorr Swiss)

Wash squash under cold running water. Remove stems from both ends. Cut zucchini in small pieces. Chop onion and tomato into small pieces.

In a heavy skillet, fry the bacon until crispy. Drain on paper towels and crumble.

In a saucepan, heat the oil. Brown the onion for 2 minutes. Add the zucchini, tomato, and chicken bouillon, then cover and let simmer about 20 minutes. Garnish with crumbled bacon. Serves 6.

CALABACITAS CON ELOTE
(Zucchini Squash with Corn)

6 zucchini squash
3 ears corn
1 red bell pepper
¼ onion

2 tbsp. corn oil
1 tsp. chicken bouillon (preferably
   Knorr Swiss)

Wash squash under cold running water. Remove stems from both ends. Cut zucchini in small pieces. Remove corn from ears. Remove stems from bell pepper and chop into small pieces. Chop onion into small pieces.

In a saucepan, heat the oil. Brown the onion for 2 minutes. Add the zucchini, corn, bell pepper, and chicken bouillon, then cover and let simmer about 20 minutes. Serves 6.

CALABACITAS CON ELOTE Y QUESO
(Zucchini Squash with Corn and Cheese)

6 zucchini squash	**2 tbsp. corn oil**
3 ears corn	**¼ cup milk**
1 tomato	**1 cup plain yogurt**
¼ onion	**1 cup Jack cheese, grated**

Preheat oven to 375 degrees F (191 degrees C).

Wash squash under cold running water. Remove stems from both ends. Cut zucchini in small pieces. Remove corn from ears. Chop tomato and onion.

In a saucepan, heat the oil. Brown the onion for 2 minutes. Add the tomato and bring to a boil. Reduce heat and let simmer 5 minutes. Add the zucchini and corn and cook another 5 minutes. Transfer to an oven-proof earthenware casserole.

Mix the milk with the yogurt until smooth. Pour over the casserole dish and sprinkle liberally with grated cheese. Bake in preheated oven for 30 minutes. Serve immediately. Serves 6.

CALABACITAS EN VINAGRE
(Marinated Zucchini Squash)

6 zucchini squash	**¼ tsp. oregano leaves**
¼ cup corn oil	**1½ cups red wine vinegar**
4 cloves garlic, whole	**Salt and pepper to taste**
1 onion, sliced in rings	

Slice unpeeled zucchini into thin rounds. Heat oil in heavy frying pan and reduce heat to medium. Sauté zucchini together with the whole cloves garlic and onion rings. Reduce heat to low, cover pan, and cook until almost all the water from the zucchini has evaporated. Remove cover after 5 to 8 minutes so remaining liquid will evaporate and if necessary add a little more corn oil. When cooked, transfer to a glass jar, cover with oregano, vinegar, salt, and pepper, and close jar tightly. Keep in refrigerator for 4 or 5 days before serving, shaking the jar now and then to be sure all the zucchini are covered with vinegar. Serves 6.

CHÍCHAROS Y ZANAHORIAS
(Peas and Carrots)

3 cups peas, fresh or frozen (not
   canned)
3 cups fresh carrots
¼ cup onion

1 tomato
¼ cup cilantro, chopped
¼ cup corn oil
1 cup water

Dice carrots. Chop onion. Slice tomato on diagonal.

In a medium saucepan, heat oil and brown onion about 1 minute. Add tomato and simmer 1 minute more. Add water, bring to a boil, reduce heat, and add peas, carrots, and cilantro. Let simmer covered about 20-25 minutes. Serves 6.

CHÍCHARO EN CACEROLA
(Pea Casserole)

1 cup water
6 cups peas, fresh or frozen (not
   canned)
4 eggs, separated
1 tbsp. sugar
6 tbsp. bread crumbs

1 cup plain yogurt
¼ cup milk
6 tbsp. butter
1 cup Jack cheese, grated
1 tsp. salt

Preheat oven to 475 degrees F (246 degrees C).

In a medium saucepan bring the water to a boil, add peas, and let cook until tender. Drain water from peas and transfer peas to blender. When cool, grind peas until they form paste.

Place egg yolks in the blender with the peas (the egg whites go in a mixing bowl to beat later). Grind pea paste with yolks. Now add the sugar, bread crumbs, yogurt, and milk and grind again. Transfer to an oven-proof earthenware casserole. Slice butter into pieces and mix into casserole with cheese. Season with salt to taste.

Beat egg whites until they are stiff (about 5 minutes). Gently fold egg whites into peas. Transfer to preheated oven and bake for 50-60 minutes. A knife inserted should come out clean when cooking is complete. Serve immediately. Serves 6.

COLIFLOR EN CACEROLA
(Cauliflower Casserole)

1 large tomato
2 cloves garlic
3 serrano chilies
2 tbsp. corn oil

1 large cauliflower
2 cups water
2 cups Jack cheese, grated

In a blender, grind the tomatoes, garlic, and chilies. Sauté this sauce in oil in a medium saucepan for 5 minutes.

Preheat oven to 350 degrees F (176 degrees C).

Rinse cauliflower and remove outer leaves. In a large saucepan bring the water to a boil. Place cauliflower in pan, reduce heat, and simmer for 15-20 minutes. Drain water and cut cauliflower in florets.

Transfer cauliflower into an earthenware casserole. Sprinkle with sauce and then garnish with grated cheese. Place in preheated oven for 10 minutes, or until cheese melts. Serves 6.

EJOTES
(String Beans)

3 strips bacon
3 cups fresh string beans
¼ cup corn oil
¼ cup onion, chopped

1 tomato, chopped
½ cup water
2 eggs, hard-boiled

In a heavy frying pan, fry the bacon. Drain on paper towels and crumble. Remove the strings from the string beans and cut off the tips. Cut the string beans in 1½-inch julienne slices by first cutting string beans into equal lengths, then cutting them into match-stick strips (i.e, ////). In a medium saucepan, heat oil and brown onion for 1 minute. Add tomato and water; let simmer for 1 minute more. Add string beans and cook for 10 minutes, or until tender. Garnish with crumbled bacon and chopped hard-boiled eggs. Serves 6.

ELOTE ROSTIZADO
(Roasted Corn)

12 ears corn
1 stick butter

6 limes, cut in wedges
Pequín chili

Preheat oven to 350 degrees F (176 degrees C).

Remove husks and silk from corn, spread with butter, and then wrap each corn in aluminum foil. Place corn in preheated oven for 1 hour.

Serve with plenty of butter, limes, and chili. Serves 6.

CACEROLA DE ELOTE
(Corn Casserole)

6 cups corn kernels, fresh or frozen
  (not canned)
¼ cup onion, chopped
1 cup Manchego or Jack cheese,
  grated
3 eggs

1 tbsp. sugar
6 tbsp. bread crumbs
1 cup plain yogurt
¼ cup milk
¼ cup corn oil
1 tsp. salt

Preheat oven to 475 degrees F (246 degrees C).

In a blender grind the eggs, sugar, bread crumbs, yogurt, and milk for 2-3 minutes.

Heat oil in a heavy frying pan and fry the chopped onion for 1 minute. Add corn and fry another 2 minutes.

Transfer sautéed corn to oven-proof earthenware casserole, pour egg mixture from blender over corn, and stir. Season with salt. Add ½ of the grated cheese and stir, pour the remaining grated cheese on top, cover, and bake for 45 minutes to 1 hour. Serves 6.

RAJAS CON CEBOLLA
(Rajas with Onion)

This recipe is a side dish as well as a garnish to numerous Mexican dishes.

6 poblano chilies
3 onions

¼ cup corn oil

On a comal roast the poblano chilies until the skins blister. Place these chilies in a cellophane bag and let sweat for 10 minutes. Remove from bag and peel skins as best you can. Remove stem and seeds from each chili; cut in strips. Set aside.

Slice the onions on the diagonal in 1-inch-thick pieces. In a heavy frying pan, fry the chilies in oil with the onions (about 15 minutes). Place in an oven-proof earthenware dish to keep warm in oven.

Accompany grilled meat with the ''rajas'' and onion on the side and a favorite Mexican rice, a favorite salsa, and plenty of tortillas. Serves 6.

PURÉ DE ESPINACAS
(Creamed Spinach)

1 lb. spinach
⅓ cup water

½ cup butter or margarine (8 tbsp.)

Rinse spinach very well. Discard stems. Place spinach leaves in a large pot with water, cover, and simmer for 15-20 minutes. When spinach is well cooked, discard water. Place spinach in a blender and grind for 2-3 minutes. Return ground spinach to pot and simmer with the butter or margarine for 5 minutes over low heat. Serves 6.

PAPAS FRITAS
(Fried Potatoes)

6 red potatoes
1 onion

¼ cup corn oil

Peel potatoes; cut potatoes and onion in thin circles. Heat oil in heavy frying pan on medium heat and fry potatoes and onion rings until crispy (about 20 minutes), stirring frequently. Serves 6.

PANQUÉS DE PAPA
(Potato Pancakes)

6 red potatoes
2 eggs, beaten
1 cup Manchego or Jack cheese,
   shredded

1 tsp. salt
1 cup bread crumbs
¼ cup corn oil

Bring water to a boil in a large pot. Peel potatoes, cut into 1-inch pieces, and put in boiling water. Reduce heat, semi-cover, and let potatoes simmer for 25-30 minutes, until fully cooked. Discard water.

Preheat oven to warm, 150 degrees F (65 degrees C).

In a 5-quart mixer, beat the potatoes on medium speed until smooth. Mix in the eggs, grated cheese, salt, and ½ cup bread crumbs. Form 1-inch balls and then flatten the balls into pancake shapes.

In a heavy frying pan, heat oil. Dip potato pancakes in remaining bread crumbs and fry potato pancakes until brown on both sides — 1 minute on each side and then 30 seconds on first side again. Place fried pancakes on an oven-proof earthenware dish, with a paper towel to absorb the excess oil. When you are finished, discard the paper and place the pancakes in the warmed oven until ready to serve. Serves 6.

BOLAS DE PAPA
(Potato Balls)

8 cups water
6 potatoes
3 eggs
1½ cups Manchego or Jack cheese,
   grated

Salt and pepper
1 cup corn oil
½ cup bread crumbs

In a large pot, bring water to a boil. Peel potatoes and quarter, drop potatoes into boiling water, and reduce heat. Simmer for 25-30 minutes, until potatoes are tender when a fork is inserted. Drain water and mash potatoes with a potato masher, electric mixer, or rotary beater.

Separate eggs and beat egg whites until stiff peaks form. Add egg yolks, cheese, salt, and pepper to the mashed potatoes and mix. Form balls.

Heat oil in heavy frying pan. Dip potato balls into the bread crumbs, then the eggs whites. Immediately fry the potato balls in the hot oil. Accompany with meat, peas, and a salad. Serves 6.

CHAPTER 16
TAMALES

Tamales are eaten at parties or special celebrations. Generally, it is the custom to gather at least two people together to assemble the tamales. As an example, you can prepare the fillings, the dough, and the husks. Your assistant then arrives to help you fill the patted-dry corn husks with the prepared masa and the filling and to seal each tamale. They are steamed for 1 to 1½ hours, or until the husks peel away easily. They are especially easy for people who like to make pastries.

The nixtamal mill *(molino de nixtamal)* is a mill that prepares the ground corn dough *(masa)* to make tortillas and tamales. In Mexico the tortillerias rely on the *molino de nixtamal* to purchase the masa to make tortillas. These tortillerias open at 10:00 A.M. and are in full swing until 4:00 P.M., but by 2:00 are generally sold out of tortillas. The Mexican housewife relies on the tortilleria for fresh daily tortillas. Since the tortillerias only have enough masa for the daily production of tortillas, the Mexican housewife, as well as eating establishments, rely on the molino de nixtamal for the fresh prepared masa for tamales. In the United States, where tortillerias are not as ubiquitous and where the tortillas are purchased at the supermarket, the nixtamal mill becomes the distributor of the tortillas as well. If prepared dough is needed for tamales, it is necessary to go early in the morning to the distributor of tortillas, in the United States generally referred to as a tortilla factory (which is really a combined nixtamal mill and tortilleria).

The best results are obtained with ready-made masa dough *(masa preparada)* from a tortilla factory. The cook simply adds the shortening, baking powder, and chicken or beef stock. The masa preparada should be ordered from the factory a day in advance for the quantity of tamales to be made.

If no tortilla factory is accessible to you, you will need to use corn masa harina purchased at a grocery store. This is a finely ground corn flour from specially treated corn. We recommend Quaker Corn Masa Harina. Do not purchase flour masa harina; the corn is the one you need. Do not be tempted to use cornmeal as a substitute.

Basic recipes using both masa preparada and the alternative masa harina are given below.

Dried husks of ears of corn, washed and soaked overnight in warm water for softness and pliability, are used to envelop the Mexican tamales from many regional areas. A couple of tablespoons of masa with the filling in the center of the spread-out masa are wrapped snugly with one or two husks. The husks are closed on the sides, then on both ends, then secured by a strip of the husks, tying both ends. The corn husks are available in plastic packages at large supermarkets and Mexican specialty shops, and can also be ordered from a tortilla factory. They keep almost indefinitely in a cool, dry place. When corn husks are unavailable, you can substitute parchment paper secured with wool string. Aluminum foil should never be used as it will impart a metallic taste to the tamales.

Alternatively, fresh banana leaves, washed and cooked only to a boiling point then removed from the stove, can be used to envelop tamales, as with the tamales Oaxaqueños from Oaxaca, Mexico and sometimes the Euchepos from Michoacan, Mexico. If banana leaves are unavailable, you can substitute parchment paper. Both must be cut into an approximate seven-by-seven-inch square. The masa dough is placed in the center with its filling, then the banana leaf is snugly folded over the dough and filling to form a square which is tied with strips of the same banana leaf on each end.

RECETA BÁSICA PARA TAMALES DE MASA PREPARADA
(Basic Recipe for "Masa Preparada" Tamales)

The preparation of tamales does not vary much from one cook to the next, except that the tamales are filled and seasoned innumerable ways. They can be filled with shrimp, chicken, beef, or pork; seasoned with red mole, green mole, salsa ranchera, or salsa verde; made sweet with anise or without anise; etc.

50 dried corn husks (about 2 pkg.)　　**1 tsp. baking powder**
1 lb. masa preparada (corn)　　　　　 **1 cup shortening**
1 cup stock　　　　　　　　　　　　　　**1 tsp. salt**

Numerous fillings are given later in this chapter.

In a large pan, clean and soak the corn husks in warm water until soft and pliable, 4-8 hours or overnight. Drain water from leaves and use immediately. With scissors, cut the points if they have not already been cut in the package.

Place masa preparada and ¼ cup stock in the bowl of a 5-quart mixer. Using the mixer's dough hook on stir speed, soften masa preparada and stock. Mix in baking powder. Continuing on stir speed, mix in shortening and beat for 4 minutes. Mix in salt and remaining stock, increase speed to medium, and beat for 4-5 minutes. Drop some dough into a cup of water — if it floats, it is ready. If it sinks, continue beating.

Place 2 husks together (making the husk wider). Spread a thin layer of dough (about 2 tablespoons) over an area of about 3 x 3 inches in the center of the husks.

Place 1 tablespoon of preferred filling (beef, chicken, etc.), then 1 tablespoon of a sauce of your choice, on top of the dough. Fold the long sides of the leaf over the dough, then fold the tips over the center, and tie shut with a thin strip of husk.

Place the tamales upright in the top of a large steamer, and cook until the dough separates easily from the leaf (about 1½ to 2 hours). (You can line the bottom of a large pot with aluminum foil, place tamales upright, and pour water into the bottom of the pot — do not let the tamales touch the water.)

Check the pot every 30 minutes to see if you need to add more water. Some cooks prefer to place a coin in the bottom of the pot because it will rattle when the water has evaporated. (The coin of course should first be sterilized.) Makes 25 tamales.

RECETA BÁSICA PARA TAMALES DE "MASA HARINA"
(Basic Recipe for "Masa Harina" Tamales)

This recipe calls for any filling that you might want to create using masa harina. First rinse husks, then make filling and sauce of your choice, then prepare masa harina dough. You can then assemble and steam tamales.

50 dried corn husks (about 2 pkg.)	**1 tsp. baking powder**
½ cup shortening	**1 tsp. salt**
4 cups masa harina (corn)	**2 cups chicken or beef stock**

Numerous fillings are given following this recipe.

In a large pan, rinse and soak the corn husks in hot water until they are soft and pliable, 4-8 hours or overnight. Drain water from husks and use immediately. With scissors, cut the points if they have not already been cut in the package.

In a 5-quart electric mixer on medium speed (with shield guard to protect against splattering), beat shortening until it is light and fluffy. Alternately mix in masa harina, baking powder, and salt with the stock, until a firm dough is formed. The dough should be moist but not wet.

Place 2 husks together (making the husk wider). Spread a thin layer of dough (about 2 tablespoons) over an area of about 3 x 3 inches in the center of the husks.

Place 1 tablespoon of preferred filling (beef, chicken, etc.), then 1 tablespoon of sauce, on top of the dough. Fold the long sides of the leaf over the dough, then fold the tips over the center, and tie shut with a thin strip of husk.

Place the tamales upright in the top of a large steamer, and cook until the dough separates easily from the leaf (about 1 to 1½ hours). (You can line the bottom of a large pot with aluminum foil, place tamales upright, and pour water into the bottom of the pot — do not let the tamales touch the water.)

Check the pot every 20 minutes to see if you need to add more water. Some cooks prefer to place a coin in the bottom of the pot because it will rattle when the water has evaporated. (The coin of course should be sterilized.) Makes 25 tamales.

FILLINGS FOR TAMALES

RELLENO DE CARNE DE RES PARA TAMALES CON SALSA RANCHERA
(Beef Filling for Tamales with Ranch Sauce)

1 recipe roasted ranch sauce (see index)
6 cloves garlic
3 lb. flank steak
½ cup corn oil
1 (12 oz.) can beer, room temperature

Prepare your roasted ranch sauce.

Put garlic through garlic press and spread over beef. Heat oil in covered skillet and brown meat uncovered. When brown on all sides, add beer and cook covered about 1 ½ to 2 hours, or until meat is tender. Remove beef from stove and let cool. When beef is cool, shred it. Use to fill tamales; top tamales with roasted ranch sauce. Makes 25 tamales.

RELLENO DE POLLO CON MOLE PARA TAMALES
(Chicken with Mole Filling for Tamales)

3-4 cups water
4 chicken breasts
1 white onion, whole
3 cloves garlic, whole
2 bay leaves
¼ cup Doña María mole paste
1 tomato
1 cup chicken stock
½ cup corn oil
Salt to taste

In heavy pot, bring the water to a boil. Add the chicken, whole onion, garlic cloves, and bay leaves. Let chicken boil covered for 5 minutes. Reduce heat and simmer for 35-45 minutes, or until meat is tender. Shred chicken.

Place mole paste in blender with tomato and chicken stock and grind until a smooth paste forms. In a heavy saucepan, simmer this sauce in oil until it thickens (about 10-15 minutes). Salt to taste. Fills 25 tamales.

RELLENO DE CARNE DE PUERCO PARA TAMALES CON SALSA VERDE
(Pork Filling for Tamales with Tomatillo Sauce)

5 cups water
2 lb. pork loin
1 large onion, whole
1 tsp. oregano

4 cloves garlic, minced
1 tsp. Maggi seasoning
1 recipe roasted tomatillo sauce
   (see index)

Bring water to a boil in a heavy pot. Add pork and whole onion, reduce heat to medium-high, and boil for 1 hour. After the hour has run, mix in oregano, minced garlic, and Maggi seasoning and simmer 30 minutes more. Let cool; shred pork. Set stock aside to use in tamale dough. Prepare sauce and use over tamales. Makes 25 tamales.

RELLENO DE CAMARONES PARA TAMALES CON SALSA PASILLA
(Shrimp Filling for Tamales with Pasilla Sauce)

1 recipe pasilla sauce (see index)
36 large fresh shrimp

1 tsp. red wine vinegar

Prepare sauce.

Shell shrimp — just push the shell with your thumb and forefinger and it will come off; leave tail intact. With a sharp knife cut along the curve in the body and remove the back vein. Rinse shrimp under cool water. Transfer shrimp to a mixing bowl filled with ice-cold water and then add the red wine vinegar. Place in the refrigerator for 10 minutes.

Drain liquid from shrimp and pat dry with paper towels. Place 1 large shrimp and 1 teaspoon of sauce on top of the tamale dough. Fold the long sides of the leaf over the dough, then fold the tips over the center, and tie shut with a thin strip of husk. Makes 25 tamales.

RELLENO DE PUERCO PARA TAMALES CHIAPANECOS
(Chiapaneco Pork Filling for Tamales)

Graciela Cameras of Chiapas, Mexico has shared her recipe for *tamales chiapanecos,* which are eaten in her southern region of the country. Flat patties are made out of the basic masa for tamales. These are filled with pork filling and closed into meatball shapes, then they are elegantly wrapped with the corn husk, tied on both ends with corn husk string, and neatly trimmed with scissors on both ends.

½ lb. green tomatillos, peeled,
   ground
2 large red tomatoes
¼ cup achiote paste
¼ cup pequín chili (optional)
1 ancho chili, deveined

1½ lb. pork roast
¼ tsp. oregano
1 stick cinnamon
2 cloves garlic, minced
1 onion, whole

Remove husks from tomatillos. Rinse under running water. Bring 2 cups water to a boil in heavy pot, reduce heat to medium-high, and boil tomatillos for 5-8 minutes. Remove stems from tomatillos, transfer to blender, and grind with the red tomatoes, achiote paste, pequín chili, deveined ancho chili, and a little water. Set aside for later use.

In a dutch oven on high heat, brown the pork, turning to brown on all sides. Then cover with hot water and boil for approximately 1 hour with the oregano, cinnamon stick, minced garlic, and whole onion. The pork must be very well cooked. Discard onion and water. Cool and shred pork. Mix the sauce with the shredded pork. Transfer to dutch oven and simmer on low-medium heat for 5-10 minutes.

Make flat patties with basic masa recipe given at beginning of this chapter. Fill with shredded pork and close all sides, forming round shapes. Transfer each filled ball to softened-dried corn husk and secure closed at each end with a strip of corn husk or wool string. Cut uneven ends of corn husk so both ends will look even and tidy.

Proceed to steam as in basic recipe given at beginning of this chapter. Makes 50 tamales.

TAMALES OAXAQUEÑOS
(Tamales from Oaxaca)

These square-shaped tamales have a unique flavor acquired from the banana leaf and mole paste.

1 basic recipe for masa harina
   tamales or masa preparada
   tamales
Banana leaves or parchment paper
   (enough for 25 7″×7″ squares)
1 turkey breast
1 onion, whole
2 cloves garlic, minced
1 bay leaf
1 tomato

¼ onion
2 cloves garlic
¼ cup Doña María mole paste
1 1-inch piece banana
½ cup almonds
¼ cup raisins
¼ cup sesame seeds
1 tsp. red wine vinegar
¼ cup turkey stock
½ tsp. salt

Prepare masa according to basic recipe for masa harina tamales or masa preparada tamales. In a large pot, boil the banana leaves for 5 minutes. Cool and cut into 7-inch by 7-inch squares. Reserve extra strips of banana leaves to tie tamales securely or use wool string.

In a dutch oven, bring 4 cups water to a boil. Place in the boiling water the turkey breast, whole onion, minced garlic, and bay leaf. Cover and cook on medium-high heat until turkey is tender, about 1 hour. Cool and shred the turkey breast.

On a hot griddle (lined with aluminum foil) on medium heat roast (turning frequently) the tomato, ¼ onion, and 2 cloves garlic. Transfer roasted ingredients to blender and grind with the mole paste, banana, almonds, raisins, sesame seeds, vinegar, ¼ cup stock, and salt. Grind until all the ingredients are smooth.

Proceed to use the banana leaves or parchment paper by placing 2 tablespoons masa dough on each banana leaf, 1 tablespoon of shredded turkey, and 1 tablespoon of mole. Close each leaf into square and secure with strip of leaf or wool string.

Steam as instructed in the basic recipe for tamales. Makes 25.

TAMALES DULCES DE ALMENDRA
(Sweet Almond Tamales)

These sweet tamales are traditionally accompanied with a sweet drink made from corn called *atole* (see index).

50 dried corn husks (about 2 pkg.)
1 cup butter or margarine
1 cup shortening
1 cup sugar
2 whole eggs, beaten
1 lb. masa preparada or masa harina
2 tsp. baking powder

1 tsp. salt
1 cup almonds
1 cup milk (use ¼ less if using masa preparada)
¾ cup raisins
1 tsp. almond extract
1 tsp. vanilla extract

First soak the corn husks. They need to be in water at least 4 to 8 hours so they will be soft. Pat dry just before using each one.

In a 5-quart electric mixer on medium speed, beat butter, shortening, and sugar until light and fluffy, about 3-5 minutes. Mix in eggs and continue beating on low.

In a mixing bowl mix masa with baking powder and salt. Grind almonds in blender until coarsely chopped.

On stir speed, mix into butter the masa alternatively with the milk. Mix in the almonds, raisins, almond extract, and vanilla. You are now ready to transfer the masa mixture to the corn husks. Secure closed with strips of corn husks or wool string.

Proceed to steam the tamales as in the basic tamale recipes. Makes 25.

Variations: You can have fun by substituting sweet condensed milk for the regular sweet milk, or changing the flavor by omitting the almond flavor and using anise seeds. Sweet tamales are like little cakes and you can flavor them like any favorite cake you like to eat. An example could be trying your hand at dried apricots and bananas in the sweet tamales. The possibilities are endless. Have fun!

EUCHEPOS DE ELOTE
(Fresh Corn Euchepos)

In Michoacan they make this popular tamale from fresh corn kernels which can be ground in your blender — really delicious.

25 dried corn husks (about 1 pkg.) or 1 roll parchment paper
5 cups fresh or frozen corn (not canned)
1 cup Muenster cheese, in small dice
½ cup shortening
1 to 2 tsp. pequín chili (or cayenne pepper)
2 tsp. anise seeds (optional)
1 cup granulated sugar
1 tsp. salt
2 eggs
1 roll wool string

Soak corn husks 4-8 hours, or overnight. If using frozen corn, thaw corn (remove from freezer 4-8 hours before using). Preheat oven to 375 degrees F (191 degrees C). Dry corn in oven for 15 minutes.

If using parchment paper cut 12 (10-inch squares) of parchment paper. In heavy medium pan, melt shortening. Add pequín chili and anise seeds to the melted shortening; cool to room temperature. In blender, mix the sugar, salt, eggs, thawed corn, and melted shortening. Grind turning on and off and scraping down sides until fully ground (about 4-5 minutes). Transfer to a mixing bowl. Add cheese.

Spoon 6-7 tablespoons of ground corn onto each corn husk or square of parchment paper. Fold husk or parchment paper closed like an envelope and secure with wool string. Transfer envelopes to a steamer and steam as in the instructions for basic tamales, about 1 to 1½ hours. Makes 12.

CHAPTER 17
THE BAKERY

The bakeries or *espigas* in Mexico have a regular schedule for removing the hot bread from the ovens, and that is where you will find people at certain hours choosing their warm *bolillos* to accompany their meals or *teleras* to make sandwiches ("tortas"). People can never resist the impulse to use their bread pincers to pile a few sweet breads on their trays for the breakfast or the evening *merienda*. There are neat mounds of all types of sweet breads, puff pastries, cakes, and cookies and as you exit in some *panaderías* you can also find shelves of sugar dolls for decorating ceremonial cakes.

Some people call the bolillos and teleras Mexico's *pan francés* (French bread) and they trace the roots to the era of Emperor Maximilian in Mexico, but if you go south to Bolivia, you find the *marraquetas,* which are identical to the bolillos. There was no French influence there, so maybe the Spanish conquistadors brought these bread recipes along in the conquest of the Americas. However, it cannot be disputed that Mexico's sweet breads have a French accent.

Teleras are made with the same dough as the bolillos but, as you will see in the recipe below, are shaped a little differently to make the delicious tortas that Mexicans love to eat at any time of the day or night. *Torterias* are open all day and part of the night.

BOLILLOS Y/O TELERAS
(Bolillos and/or Teleras)

1 cup warm water (105-15 degrees
  F or 41-46 degrees C)
1 envelope dry yeast
1 tbsp. sugar
⅔ cup vegetable shortening, melted

1 tsp. salt, or to taste
5 cups all-purpose flour
1 cup warm water
3 tsp. salt
¼ cup water

Measure 1 cup warm water into bowl of heavy-duty electric mixer. Sprinkle yeast and sugar over; stir with mixer for 30 seconds. Turn off and let stand until foamy, about 5 minutes.

On stir speed, using paddle attachment, mix melted vegetable shortening into yeast mixture then mix in 1 teaspoon salt and 2 cups flour, mix 2 minutes. Replace paddle with dough hook. On stir speed, mix in remaining flour alternately with 1 cup water, beat 2 minutes, increase speed to medium, and beat 3 minutes.

Oil hands and transfer dough to floured surface. Knead until elastic. Grease large bowl with 2 tablespoons oil. Add dough, turning to coat entire surface. Cover and let rise in warm draft-free area until double in volume, about 1½ hours. To test if fully risen, press 2 fingers into dough; indentations will remain. If indentations do not remain, let rise longer. Punch dough down and divide into 12 pieces.

Preheat oven to 350 degrees F (176 degrees C). Grease 2 cookie sheets.

For Bolillos: Shape each piece into an oblong shape and stretch the edges slightly to make 2 pointed tips. Holding the 2 tips, roll the dough in the air, twisting it, to shape 2 round tips on both ends. Place on prepared baking tray and make 1 incision on the top. Repeat same procedure for remaining rolls. Let rise 45 minutes before baking.

For Teleras: Shape each piece into an oblong shape and place on the prepared cookie sheets. Press slightly to flatten dough and score twice on top. Repeat procedure for remaining rolls. Let rise 45 minutes before baking.

Dissolve 3 teaspoons salt in ¼ cup water and use to brush tops of rolls. Bake in preheated oven for 30-45 minutes or until golden brown. Makes 12.

CONCHAS

These pastries are decorated with a sugar topping to look like seashells. They are a daily favorite throughout Mexico. If you are in Mexico, the shell-pattern cutter can be found in markets such as the Merced.

1 envelope yeast	5 cups flour
¼ cup warm water (105-15 degrees F or 41-46 degrees C)	¾ cup milk, room temperature
	¾ cup sugar
2 tbsp. sugar	1 cup vegetable shortening
½ cup butter, softened	1 egg yolk
⅔ cup sugar	1 cup flour
6 egg yolks, beaten	3 tsp. vanilla
1 tsp. salt	¼ cup unsweetened cocoa

In a small saucepan, dissolve yeast in warm water with sugar. In a 5-quart electric mixer on stir speed, cream butter and sugar until light and fluffy. Stir in egg yolks and salt. Alternately mix in flour and milk until all used up; mix until dough is elastic. Transfer to a greased bowl and let rise until double in bulk, about 2 hours. Punch down and place in a plastic bag; transfer to refrigerator 8 hours, or overnight.

In a 5-quart electric mixer, using paddle attachment on stir speed, mix ¾ cup sugar and vegetable shortening until light and fluffy. Add 1 egg yolk and 1 cup flour and mix about 4 minutes. Mix in vanilla. Remove half of the sugar topping from the mixing bowl to another bowl. In a cup, add some cold water to the cocoa until dissolved. On stir speed, mix unsweetened dissolved cocoa into the remaining topping. Place vanilla topping in one bowl and chocolate topping in another bowl; cover with plastic bag and place in refrigerator until ready to use. Divide the sugar topping into 24 walnut-size balls. With a rolling pin, flatten into tortilla shapes.

Preheat oven to 350 degrees F (176 degrees C). Grease 2 cookie sheets.

Divide dough into 16 egg-size balls. Transfer to prepared cookie sheets, allowing space between each ball for expansion.

Place a sugar tortilla shape on top of each egg-sized dough ball. With a sharp knife cut seashell designs both lengthwise and widthwise on sugar topping. Set aside and allow the conchas to rise again until doubled. The sugar topping will cover the conchas as they rise. Bake in preheated oven for 10-15 minutes or until shells are golden. Makes 12 vanilla conchas and 12 chocolate conchas.

MASA DE HOJALDRE
(Puff Pastry)

Some of the pastries in this book are made with puff pastry. This is our easy version. The only two rules are: work quickly and keep the ingredients chilled.

4 cups all-purpose flour
1 tsp. salt
1 lb. (4 sticks) butter, cold

1 tsp. lime juice
1 cup ice water

In a 5-quart electric mixer, mix in flour and salt. Attach flat blade. Cut the cold butter into small ½-inch cubes (refrigerate if it gets soft) and drop into flour. Mix on stir speed, 4-5 minutes. Continue on stir and mix in lime juice and ice water until they have been absorbed by the flour, 1 minute only. Dough will be a rough mass. Chill dough in the refrigerator for 20 minutes.

Place the dough on a lightly floured work surface. With the palms push it into a rough rectangle. Brush with flour. With a rolling pin roll into a 12-inch rectangle, ½ inch thick. Fold rectangle over 3 times (it should look like a folded package) and refrigerate 20 minutes.

Remove from refrigerator and roll into another rectangle 12 inches long. Fold over 3 times and refrigerate for 20 minutes more.

Remove from refrigerator and roll into a rectangle 12 inches long again. Fold over 3 times and refrigerate for 20 minutes.

Transfer dough to a plastic wrap and chill dough for 8 hours or overnight. Can rest in refrigerator up to 3 days. Makes approximately 3 pounds.

EMPANADAS DE FIESTA
(Party Empanadas)

These sweet and savory empanadas will disappear first at any buffet or party. The day before, just make the easy puff pastry recipe given above, then the next day fill it with your favorite filling and fold closed. We fill ours with a slice of quince *ate* (see index) and a slice of Manchego cheese (or Gruyère). Most Latin American specialty stores have ates for sale.

1½ lb. puff pastry (see above)
1 roll parchment paper

1 quince *ate* (see index)
1 Manchego or Gruyère cheese

Preheat oven to 425 degrees F (218 degrees C).

Using a rolling pin, roll the dough until it forms a 12-inch square, ⅛ inch thick. With a sharp knife, trim edges. Place in freezer 5 minutes. Remove from freezer, bring the 2 ends of the dough toward the center, and fold lengthwise.

Now fold again lengthwise toward center to make a 4-layer dough 12 inches wide. Transfer to freezer for 5 minutes. Remove from freezer.

Line 2 cookie sheets with parchment paper.

With a 6-inch round cutter or lid to a pan, cut rounds until all the dough has been used up. Fill each round with a slice of ate and a slice of cheese, then fold closed. Lay them on cookie sheets lined with parchment paper in staggered rows, about 2 inches apart. Return to freezer 5 minutes.

Bake in the preheated oven for 25-30 minutes, or until golden. Transfer empanadas to a wire rack to cool. Serve immediately or same day. Makes 24 6-inch empanadas.

OREJITAS
(Little Ears)

These *orejitas* are a favorite with everyone who goes to the bakery.

1 roll parchment paper   **½ cup confectioners' sugar**
1½ lb. puff pastry (see above)

Line 2 cookie sheets with parchment paper. Preheat oven to 425 degrees F (218 degrees C).

Using a rolling pin, roll the dough over the sugar until it forms a 12-inch square, ⅛ inch thick. With a sharp knife, trim edges. Place in freezer 5 minutes. Remove from freezer and brush both sides of dough with confectioners' sugar.

Bring the 2 ends of the dough toward the center and fold lengthwise.

Now fold again lengthwise toward center to make a 4-layer dough 12 inches wide. Brush both sides of the dough with more confectioners' sugar. Place in freezer again for 5 minutes. Remove from freezer.

With a sharp knife, cut pastry into thin strips, ¼ inch wide by 3½ inches across, then close each pastry strip to form butterfly shape or ears. Lay them on cookie sheets lined with parchment paper in staggered rows, about 2 inches apart. Return to freezer for 5 minutes.

Bake in the preheated oven for 25-30 minutes, or until golden. Transfer orejitas to a wire rack to cool. They will be sticky so do not place one on top of the other. Serve immediately or same day. Makes 24.

CUERNITOS DULCES
(Little Sweet Horns)

This Mexican favorite sweet bread is made daily at many of the bakeries. One wonders if Maximillian and Carlota brought the recipe with them when they arrived in Mexico.

1 roll parchment paper   **½ cup confectioners' sugar**
1½ lb. puff pastry (see above)

Line 2 cookie sheets with parchment paper. Preheat oven to 425 degrees F (218 degrees C).

Using a rolling pin, roll the dough over the sugar until it forms a 12-inch square, ⅛ inch thick. With a sharp knife, trim edges. Place in freezer for 5 minutes. Remove from freezer, roll out, fold the 2 ends of the dough toward the center, and fold lengthwise.

Now fold again lengthwise toward center to make a 4-layer dough 12 inches wide. Place in freezer again for 5 minutes. Remove from freezer.

With a sharp knife, cut pastry into 4-inch-wide triangles, then roll the pastry closed to form "horns." Lay the horns on cookie sheets lined with parchment paper in staggered rows, about 2 inches apart. Return to freezer for 5 minutes.

Bake in the preheated oven for 25-30 minutes, or until golden. Transfer cuernitos to a wire rack to cool. Serve immediately or same day. Makes 24.

CHAPTER 18
DESSERTS

Like any other people in the Western world, Mexicans love to have dessert after their principal meal. Dessert customs vary from region to region and according to social status. In Mexico City, people would rather have a flan or piece of cake accompanied by a cup of coffee, while in the provinces they might have a variety of fruit cut into pieces, a regional pastry, sweet bread, or a piece of *ate* with coffee.

FLAN AUTÉNTICO
(Authentic Flan)

½ cup sugar
6 egg yolks
3 eggs, whole
1 cup sugar

2 tbsp. cornstarch
1 tsp. vanilla
3 cups milk

Preheat oven to 375 degrees F (191 degrees C).

Place individual 1-cup Pyrex molds in a 1-inch-deep rectangular pan. Pour boiling water into pan, being careful not to wet clean molds.

In a heavy skillet, measure ½ cup sugar (to caramelize) and cook on medium-low heat until it turns caramel color — immediately pour caramelized sugar into bottom of clean molds. If sugar hardens on you, reheat briefly and it will melt again. Set aside while you prepare the flan. (You can clean skillet by boiling water in it.)

Prepare Flan: In a 5-quart electric mixer on medium-high speed, beat egg yolks, whole eggs, 1 cup sugar, cornstarch and vanilla until light yellow and fluffy, about 5 minutes. Stir in milk and then transfer this mixture to custard cups, filling ¾ full. Bake in preheated oven about 1½ hours, or until flan is golden colored. Do not underbake. Carefully remove from oven (do not drop boiling water on yourself; may let cool in open oven that has been turned off) and let come to room temperature. Refrigerate molds and serve when cold.

To unmold, place chilled flan molds in a pan with boiling water. This will melt and loosen caramel. Then invert on individual plates. Makes 6 1-cup flans.

Flan with Cream Cheese: For this variation, bring a 4-ounce package of cream cheese to room temperature. Beat it until fluffy with the sugar, eggs, and cornstarch, then mix in the milk and vanilla and bake as for Authentic Flan.

Kahlúa Flan: Proceed to make Authentic Flan, only substitute ½ cup Kahlúa for ½ cup of the milk in the flan.

Sweet Flan: Omit regular milk and replace with sweet condensed milk, ½ cup water, and ¼ cup sugar. Otherwise proceed as with Authentic Flan.

Flan with Coconut: Proceed to make Authentic Flan, only just before pouring into the sugar-coated molds, mix in 1½ cups flaked coconut.

ARROZ CON LECHE
(Rice Pudding)

3 cups evaporated milk
½ cup sugar
2 sticks cinnamon, 3 inches long
4 tbsp. butter or margarine
4 cups water

2 cups long-grain rice
½ cup raisins
Salt to taste
Ground cinnamon

In a medium saucepan on medium heat, cook first four ingredients until the mixture thickens (about 30 minutes), stirring frequently.

Bring water to a boil and mix in rice, raisins, and salt. Let boil 1 minute, reduce heat to low, cover, and let simmer until fully cooked (20 minutes). Turn heat off, but leave rice on burner so it will become fluffy.

Preheat oven to 350 degrees F. In an oven-proof casserole, mix cooked rice with milk, transfer to heated oven, and bake for 20 minutes. Discard cinnamon sticks. Serve warm or cold sprinkled with cinnamon. Serves 6.

EMPANADAS DE DULCE DE ATE
(Sweet-Ate Empanadas)

We dedicate this recipe to our very favorite tenor, Placido Domingo. We have heard that he loves *ate* and cheese together in a torta.

½ cup vegetable shortening
2 tbsp. sugar
1 egg yolk
2 cups flour
1 tsp. baking powder

½ tsp. salt
¼ cup ice-cold water
1 recipe quince *ate* (see index)
1 cup Gruyère cheese, grated

In a 5-quart electric mixer on medium speed, cream shortening and sugar. Mix in egg yolk. On stir speed, mix in flour, baking powder, and salt alternately with ice-cold water. Increase speed to medium and beat for 3-4 minutes only. Transfer to an unfloured board and knead 1 minute until smooth. Transfer to cellophane bag and refrigerate for 8 hours, or overnight.

Preheat oven to 375 degrees F (191 degrees C). Form dough into 12 balls and flatten the balls to saucer shapes. Fill with 1 slice quince *ate* and a small portion of grated cheese, fold in half to close, and with your thumb and forefinger twist the seam closed. Make sure they are sealed or the juice will escape. Bake 10-15 minutes at 425 degrees F (218 degrees C) or until dough is golden.

Other fillings that are a favorite include blackberry jelly, apricot jelly, or marmalade, whichever is your preference. Makes 12.

POLVORONES
(Mexican Cookies)

This popular Mexican party cookie is so delicious that we have been asked to include it here.

1 cup (2 sticks) butter, room temperature	½ tsp. salt
½ cup sugar	1 tsp. cinnamon, ground
1 tsp. vanilla	1 cup pecans, chopped
2¼ cups flour	¼ cup confectioners' sugar

In a 5-quart electric mixer on medium speed, beat butter until light and fluffy. On stir speed, mix in sugar and vanilla. Continue on stir speed and mix in flour, salt, cinnamon, and chopped pecans until well blended (add 2 tablespoons ice water if needed). The dough will be stiff. Transfer dough to a plastic bag and refrigerate 4-8 hours, or overnight. Remove from refrigerator 1-2 hours before using (so dough will soften).

Preheat oven to 400 degrees F (204 degrees C). Shape dough into 1-inch balls. Place on ungreased cookie sheets. Bake for approximately 25 minutes (do not underbake). Roll warm cookies in confectioners' sugar; cool completely. Once cookies are cold roll in confectioners' sugar one last time. Wrap in 8-by-8-inch white tissue paper, if desired. Tie each end with string and trim ends. If Christmastime use red/green tissue paper. Makes 42.

GALLETITAS DE CACAHUATE
(Peanut Cookies)

1 cup peanuts
1 cup butter, room temperature
1 cup white sugar
1 cup brown sugar

2 eggs
2 ⅔ cups flour
1 tsp. baking soda
¼ tsp. salt

Preheat oven to 375 degrees F (191 degrees C). On a cookie sheet lined with aluminum foil, roast the peanuts 10 minutes, turning to roast all sides. Remove from oven and cool. In a blender, grind peanuts. Set aside.

In a 5-quart electric mixer on medium speed, cream butter and sugars until light and fluffy. On stir speed, mix in eggs, flour, baking soda, salt, and peanuts until well blended. With a teaspoon, drop spoonfuls onto ungreased cookie sheets. Bake at 350 degrees F (176 degrees C) for 15 minutes, or until golden. Transfer to cookie rack to cool. Makes 42.

PASTEL DE PISTACHE
(Pistachio Cake)

This is a beautiful cake. If you are preparing it for a very special occasion, you may want to make the candied limes (see index).

1½ cups pistachios
½ cup pistachios
12 whole pistachios
½ cup butter or margarine
1½ cups sugar
8 oz. cream cheese, beaten
4 eggs
1½ cups flour
1 tsp. baking powder
1 tsp. baking soda
½ tsp. salt
¼ cup milk, with 1 drop lime
¼ cup lime juice

¼ cup Grand Marnier
4 drops green vegetable food color
4 tbsp. cornstarch
½ cup water
1 cup sugar
1 tsp. salt
3 egg yolks, beaten
1 cup lime juice
4 tbsp. butter or margarine
4 tbsp. Grand Marnier
8 oz. cream cheese
2 cups confectioners' sugar

Pistachios can be peeled by boiling 3 minutes to remove skins. Roast in 350 degrees F (176 degrees C) oven and cool. Finely grind 1½ cups for cake and coarsely grind ½ cup for decoration on the sides of frosting, reserving 12 whole pistachios for decorating the top of cake.

Preheat oven to 350 degrees F (176 degrees C). Prepare 3 9-inch pans by greasing and lining bottoms with parchment paper. In a 5-quart mixer, on mix speed, cream ½ cup butter and 1½ cups sugar until light and fluffy. Add 8 ounces cream cheese and continue on mix speed until light. Mix in 4 eggs one at a time and continue on mix speed 2 minutes more. Combine flour with 1½ cups pistachios, baking powder, baking soda, and ½ teaspoon salt. To butter mixture, add milk with the 1 drop of lime juice and the ¼ cup lime juice. On stir speed, alternately mix in ½ cup dry ingredients with 4 tablespoons liquid at a time until all used up. Mix in Grand Marnier and color. Transfer batter to prepared cake pans and bake for 25 minutes. Cool cakes on cake racks.

In a heavy pan dissolve cornstarch in ½ cup water with sugar and salt. Using a whisk, beat in 3 egg yolks. Stir in 1 cup lime juice and add 4 tablespoons butter. On medium heat, bring to just boiling point, reduce heat to low, and simmer, stirring constantly, about 5 minutes. Mix in Grand Marnier. Remove from heat and refrigerate. Before making frosting, spread this filling on top of first and second layers of cake. The top layer will be frosted.

In a mixing bowl, beat cream cheese until softened, add confectioners' sugar, and continue beating until light and fluffy. Spread over entire cake. Sprinkle the ½ cup coarsely ground pistachios around sides of cake. With a decorating bag, pipe some frosting on top of cake. Arrange 12 whole pistachios on top of cake and surround with candied lime peel if desired (see index). Serves 12.

PASTEL DE MANGO
(Mango Cake)

Marilyn created this cake for the children of Mexico who love mangos and above all the Manila mangos.

1½ cups canned mango
½ cup mango nectar (juice)
2 tbsp. lime juice
½ cup butter or margarine
1½ cups white sugar
4 egg yolks
2¼ cups flour
1 tsp. baking powder
1 tsp. baking soda
½ tsp. salt

4 egg whites
4 tbsp. cornstarch
2½ cups mango nectar (juice)
¾ cup granulated sugar
3 egg yolks, beaten
2 tbsp. lime juice
3 tbsp. butter, salted
1 tsp. vanilla
½ cup confectioners' sugar

Preheat oven to 350 degrees F (176 degrees C). Grease 3 9-inch round cake pans, line bottoms with parchment paper, and set pans aside. Transfer mangos to blender with ½ cup mango nectar and 2 tablespoons lime juice. Puree for 1 minute; set aside. In a 5-quart mixing bowl on medium speed, beat butter and sugar until light and fluffy, mix in egg yolks one at a time, then add in mango puree. In a mixing bowl, combine the flour, baking powder, baking soda and salt. Add flour mixture to mango mixture 1 cup at a time.

In another mixing bowl using a rotary beater, beat egg whites until stiff peaks form. Fold egg whites into cake batter. Transfer batter to prepared cake pans and bake for 25 minutes. Cool cakes on cake racks.

In a saucepan dissolve cornstarch in ½ cup of the mango nectar with sugar. Using a whisk, beat in 3 egg yolks. Stir in remaining mango nectar and lime juice and add 3 tablespoons butter. On medium heat, bring to just boiling point, reduce heat to low, and simmer, stirring constantly, for 5 minutes. Stir in vanilla. Refrigerate at least 4 hours. Cover first and second layers of cake with this mango filling.

Dust top of cake with confectioners' sugar using a sieve. Serves 12.

PASTEL DE NARANJA
(Orange Cake)

1¼ cups almonds
1¼ cups flour
1 tsp. baking powder
1 tsp. baking soda
½ tsp. salt
½ cup butter or margarine
¾ cup white sugar
¾ cup light brown sugar, packed
   loosely
4 egg yolks
2 tbsp. orange rind, finely grated
1 cup orange juice

1 tsp. vanilla extract
4 egg whites
4 tbsp. cornstarch
2 cups orange juice
¼ cup lime juice
½ tsp. salt
¾ cup granulated sugar
3 egg yolks, beaten
3 tbsp. butter or margarine
1 tsp. vanilla extract
4 tbsp. sugar
½ cup fresh orange juice

Preheat oven to 350 degrees F (176 degrees C). Grease 3 9-inch round cake pans and line bottoms with parchment paper. In blender, grind almonds. In bowl, combine almonds, flour, baking powder, baking soda, and ½ teaspoon salt. In 5-quart electric mixer, beat ½ cup butter and the white and brown sugars until light and fluffy. Mix in 4 egg yolks and the orange rind. Stir in flour mixture alternately with 1 cup orange juice and 1 teaspoon vanilla, until smooth. Using an electric hand beater, beat egg whites in a bowl until stiff; fold into cake batter. Spoon batter into pans. Bake in preheated oven 25 minutes, or until golden. Let cakes cool.

In saucepan dissolve cornstarch in 2 cups orange juice and the lime juice with salt and ¾ cup granulated sugar. Using whisk, beat in 3 egg yolks. Add 3 tablespoons butter. On medium-high heat, bring to boiling point, reduce heat to medium-low and simmer, stirring constantly, 5-8 minutes. Stir in 1 teaspoon vanilla extract; simmer 1 minute. Refrigerate 1 hour.

In a cup dissolve 4 tablespoons sugar in ½ cup fresh orange juice. Cover the 2 cake layers with the refrigerated filling. With pastry brush, moisten top and sides with orange syrup. Serves 12.

PASTEL DE CHABACANO Y PLÁTANO
(Apricot-Banana Cake)

6 oz. sun-dried apricots
1 cup water
¾ cup almonds
1½ cups flour
1 tsp. baking powder
1 tsp. baking soda
½ tsp. salt
½ cup butter or margarine
¾ cup white sugar
¾ cup dark brown sugar
3 eggs
¼ cup milk with 1 drop lime juice
2 medium bananas

2 tbsp. lime juice
1 tsp. vanilla
4 tbsp. cornstarch
2½ cups evaporated milk
1 cup granulated sugar
½ tsp. salt
2 egg yolks, beaten
3 tbsp. butter
1 tsp. vanilla
¼ tsp. banana extract
2 bananas
½ cup confectioners' sugar

Preheat oven to 350 degrees F (176 degrees C). Grease 3 9-inch round cake pans, line bottoms with parchment paper, and set pans aside. Place sun-dried apricots in a saucepan, pour the water on top, bring to a boil, reduce heat, and simmer 10 minutes. Drain liquid and finely chop apricots. In blender grind almonds and set aside. In a mixing bowl combine flour, ground almonds, baking powder, baking soda, and ½ teaspoon salt. Set aside. In a 5-quart mixing bowl beat ½ cup butter and white and brown sugars until light and fluffy; beat in 3 eggs one at a time. Next alternately add sour milk and flour until all used up. With a fork, lightly mash 2 bananas and mix into batter, then mix into batter the chopped apricots with lime juice. Mix in vanilla. Transfer batter to prepared cake pans and bake for 25 minutes. Cool cakes on cake racks.

In a heavy pan dissolve cornstarch in ½ cup evaporated milk, 1 cup granulated sugar, and ½ teaspoon salt. Using a whisk, beat in 2 egg yolks. Stir in remaining milk; add 3 tablespoons butter. On medium heat, bring to just boiling point, reduce heat to low and simmer, stirring constantly, about 5 minutes. Remove from heat and add vanilla and banana extract. Refrigerate for 2-4 hours.

Slice 2 bananas into rounds and distribute over top of first layer of cake. Cover with refrigerated banana filling, repeat this procedure for second layer of cake. Dust the top of the cake with confectioners' sugar using a sieve. Serves 6.

Variations: Substitute ground roasted peanuts for the almonds in the cake. Use coconut instead of apricots.

CHURROS

It is evident that *churros,* also called *churros Españoles,* were introduced to Mexico by the Spaniards. They are popular throughout all of Latin America.

3 cups flour
1 tsp. salt
12 tsp. sugar
2 tsp. baking powder
1½ cups water, boiling hot

2 large eggs
Corn oil for deep frying
1 lime skin
Sugar

In a 5-quart electric mixer, combine flour, salt, 12 teaspoons sugar, and baking powder. On stir speed, add boiling hot water all at once. Continue on stir speed until a smooth dough is formed. Increase speed to medium and mix in eggs, one at a time. Increase speed to high and beat 3 minutes, until the dough becomes smooth and elastic. Transfer dough to a heavy saucepan on warm heat and stir with a spoon until dough releases from the side of the pan, about 3-5 minutes. Remove dough from stove.

In a heavy frying pan, heat oil until very hot, 390 degrees F (199 degrees C) on a frying thermometer. Slice lime skin in quarters and add to hot oil (this gives the *churros* a distinct flavor). Force the dough through a pastry tube or large funnel, and fry in oil with the lime skins in 4-inch-long strips until golden. Drain on paper towels. Roll in sugar. (You can also roll in cinnamon if desired.)

Serve warm *churros* with hot chocolate. Makes 24.

BUÑUELOS

These buñuelos are generally eaten at Christmastime, but every Latin American country has its own version of these fritters. They are shaped like tortillas and fried like giant cookies.

1 (¼ oz.) packet yeast
¼ cup warm milk (105-15 degrees F
   or 41-46 degrees C)
¼ cup sugar
¼ cup butter, room temperature
¼ cup vegetable shortening

1 tsp. salt
4 cups flour
½ cup milk, warm
2 cups corn oil
1 cup sugar
1 tsp. cinnamon

In a 5-quart electric mixer, dissolve yeast in ¼ cup warm milk with ¼ cup sugar, about 5 minutes. On stir speed with shield protector, mix in butter and vegetable shortening and beat until well mixed, about 2 minutes. On stir speed, mix in salt and all the flour (1 cup at a time) alternately with ½ cup warm milk, until dough forms a light paste. Transfer to greased bowl and let rise until double in size. Punch down, transfer to plastic bag, and place in refrigerator for 8 hours or overnight.

Divide dough into 1-inch balls. On a lightly floured board, using a rolling pin, flatten the balls to 5-inch rounds. Heat oil in a wide deep fryer and fry rounds in very hot oil, turning once. Transfer to platter with paper towels to drain off excess oil. Sprinkle with 1 cup sugar and the cinnamon. Makes 24.

CHAPTER 19
CANDIES AND SWEETS

The Spanish conquest throughout the American continent brought with it the missions and convents of brothers and nuns. Among their holy duties were practicing the art of making *dulces* or confections (the nuns) and distilling liquors (the brothers). The brothers as well as the nuns took care of orphans, who would help in the preparation of candies and the work in the distilleries. Those who did not enter into the service of the Lord, as novices, left having learned the art and would dedicate themselves to their own small candy businesses. We have provided you with some of these candy recipes.

The preparation of candy needs a lot of care. Never cook candy when the humidity is high or when there is a draft. The sugar will sweat and become sticky. Sugar requires a hot, dry climate. If you do not have a sugar pan, use a pressure cooker pot because it has a thick bottom, high rims, and a handle, it conducts heat rapidly, and it holds the syrup well.

DULCE DE LECHE
(Milk Fudge)

Mexican children grow up eating this milk fudge. Take a kitchen stool or bar stool into the kitchen and get comfortable. This recipe will be a welcome sight to those Mexicans who no longer live in Mexico.

4 cups milk
1 pinch baking soda
2½ cups sugar

1 stick cinnamon
1 cup pine nuts or pecans, chopped
Confectioners' sugar

In a 4-quart pressure cooker pot on medium heat, boil the milk, soda, sugar and cinnamon stick, stirring continuously, until mixture forms a soft ball, about 1½ hours (234-40 degrees F or 112-16 degrees C; in cold water, syrup forms a soft ball that flattens when removed from water). Mix in pine nuts or pecans. Remove from heat, transfer to 5-quart electric mixer, and beat with wire whisk for 3-5 minutes. The candy will form a warm paste. Quickly transfer to pastry tube while still warm. Pass through the pastry tube, cutting candies off in 3-inch lengths, onto a board dusted with confectioners' sugar. Transfer candies to dry container. Makes 12 candies, 3 inches long and 1 inch wide.

DULCES DE COCO
(Golden Coconut Candies)

This is a convent recipe that merits taking a kitchen stool or bar stool into the kitchen before you start. It is one of our favorite candies!

2½ cups coconut, shredded
1¼ cups sugar
½ cup water
1 stick cinnamon

2 tbsp. butter
3 egg yolks
2 cups milk

Preheat oven to 375 degrees F (191 degrees C), place coconut on cookie sheet lined with aluminum foil, and roast for 15 minutes, turning with spatula occasionally to brown on all sides. Cool and set aside. Grease 8-by-8-inch square cake mold, line with parchment paper, and grease paper.

In a 4-quart pressure cooker pot, combine sugar, water, stick of cinnamon, and butter. Cook over low heat, stirring gently, until sugar dissolves. Cover and cook over medium heat 2 to 3 minutes to wash down sugar crystals from sides of pan. Uncover, stir in shredded coconut and, when it appears transparent, add the egg yolks beaten with the milk. Beat, stirring constantly, until the bottom of the pan is visible. Transfer into prepared cake pan.

Preheat oven to 375 degrees F (191 degrees C). Bake candy 45 minutes, or until golden brown. Remove from oven and let cool (1 day). Cut into squares and wrap with cellophane paper. Place candy in an airtight container which you have carefully prepared beforehand with parchment paper lining the bottom. Seal the container tightly and put in a dry place. Your candy will keep for several weeks before you use it. Makes 24 1-inch squares.

ALFAJORES DE COCO
(Coconut Alfajor Candies)

This delicacy originated in Colima, a Mexican state on the Pacific coast. For those who cannot buy this candy, here is the recipe.

30 pastry wafers	**2 cups water**
5 cups coconut, shredded	**1 stick cinnamon**
4 tbsp. water	**Red vegetable coloring**
4 cups sugar	

Grease 8-by-8-inch square cake mold and line with pastry wafers. In a blender, grind the shredded coconut with 4 tablespoons water into a fine paste.

In a 4-quart pressure cooker pot, combine sugar, 2 cups water, and stick of cinnamon. Cook over low heat, stirring gently, until sugar dissolves. Cover and cook over medium heat 2 to 3 minutes to wash down sugar crystals from sides of pan. Uncover; continue cooking to soft ball stage (234-40 degrees F or 112-16 degrees C; in cold water, syrup forms a soft ball that flattens when removed from water). Remove from heat and mix in ground coconut. Transfer to 5-quart electric mixing bowl and beat with paddle attachment on medium speed until mixture forms a paste. Divide in half; add a few drops of red vegetable coloring to one portion and leave the other white.

Fill cake mold half full with the white coconut mixture and then top with the pink coconut mixture. Let cool in dry covered container, 1 day. Slice into approximately 6-inch-long, 2-inch-wide oblong shapes. Wrap in cellophane paper and store in dry container until ready to eat. Will keep up to 3-4 weeks. Makes 4 6-inch rectangles.

ROLLO DE NUEZ
(Nut Roll)

2 cups milk
½ cup cream
1 cup sugar
2 tbsp. butter
1 vanilla pod

1 tbsp. Karo corn syrup
1 pinch baking soda
1 cup pecans, chopped
¼ cup Karo corn syrup
1 cup pecans, halves

In a 4-quart pressure cooker on medium heat, boil the milk, cream, sugar, butter, vanilla, and 1 tablespoon corn syrup. Cook until the mixture begins to thicken, then add the soda and continue cooking until it reaches the soft ball stage, about 1½ hours (234-40 degrees F or 112-16 degrees C; in cold water, syrup forms a soft ball that flattens when removed from water). Mix in chopped pecans. Remove from heat, transfer to 5-quart electric mixer, and beat with wire whisk for 3-5 minutes. The candy will form a warm paste.

On a board knead and roll the paste into 2 rolls. Cover lightly with ¼ cup corn syrup and then with the pecan halves placed close together so as to cover the whole candy rolls. Let harden in a tightly closed container. Can be stored in airtight container. Makes 2 rolls, 4 inches long and 4 inches thick.

CAMOTES DULCES DE SANTA CLARA
(Santa Clara Sweet Potato Candies)

1 lb. sweet potatoes
1 cup sugar

1 cup water

Wash and scrub sweet potatoes. In pressure cooker, cook 10 minutes. Let cool, peel, mash, and pass through a sieve. Set aside.

In pressure cooker pot on low heat dissolve sugar with the water, cover, and simmer 2-3 minutes to wash down crystals from sides of pan. Uncover and continue cooking on medium heat to firm ball stage (242-48 degrees F or 112-16 degrees C; in cold water, syrup forms a firm ball that does not flatten when removed from water).

Add the potatoes to the syrup. Let cook until the mixture resembles a paste. Remove from heat and using a 5-quart mixer on low speed, beat with paddle attachment until cool. By hand, roll bits of paste into 1-inch-thick by 3-inch-long sticks. Place them on a board covered with waxed paper and let them dry in a warm dry place, 1 day. The following day, once dry, brush the candies with glaze below. Dry again. Wrap individual candies in waxed paper or tissue paper.

GLAZE

1 cup sugar   **¼ cup water**

Boil sugar with water to the thread stage, 234 degrees F (112 degrees C). Syrup spins 2-inch thread when dropped from a spoon. Remove from heat and apply with a pastry brush to the candies. Makes 32.

CAJETA DE CELAYA
(Celaya Cajeta)

Get comfortable on a kitchen stool or bar stool to make this delicacy. It takes about one hour and it will be fun if you are comfortable.

1 pinch baking soda   **3 cups goat's milk**
3 tsp. cornstarch   **1½ cups sugar**
3 cups cow's milk   **1 1-qt. jar with lid**

Dissolve soda and corn starch in 1 cup cow's milk. Heat the goat's milk and remaining cow's milk to a boiling point, then add the soda and cornstarch solution. Add the sugar and continue cooking. Stir constantly with a wooden spoon until the bottom of the pan can be seen. Remove from flame and pour into a 1-quart sterilized jar.

CAJETA CON VINO
(Cajeta with Wine)

5 tbsp. sherry

Prepare *cajeta* as described above, but add sherry when the mixture has cooked to the point where the bottom of the pan is visible.

MEMBRILLATE
(Quince Paste)

Ates are sweet fruit pastes which can be found throughout Latin America. In English, *ates* are called *sweetsop*. The *ates* are nothing more than the mixing of equal amounts of fruit pulp and sugar, forming a fruit paste. One of the most common in Mexico is "membrill*ate*" (*ate* of quince) and the same one can be found in Bolivia, with the name of *carne de membrillo* (quince meat). Other popular fruits used in the preparation of *ates* due to their abundance are: guavas, mangos, pineapples, peaches, and plums. You should try a slice of cheese with *ate* some time.

1 lb. quinces   **2½ cups sugar**

Line an 8-by-8-inch square cake pan with cellophane paper. Set aside.

Peel and core the quinces and soak them briefly in salt water, then rinse. Soak the cores in 1½ cups water for 2 hours; strain core water through sieve (to obtain pectin). In a pressure cooker pot, boil quinces in 2 cups fresh water and the strained core water until quinces soften, about 20 minutes.

In a blender, grind quinces and pass through a sieve; set aside. Strain reserved liquid; set aside.

In a medium pot, boil sugar in 1 cup water to the soft ball stage (234-40 degrees F or 112-16 degrees C; in cold water, syrup forms a soft ball that flattens when removed from water).

Mix in the sieved quince and the sieved reserved liquid. Continue cooking over medium heat until the quince mixture thickens and will not stick to the sides of the pot. Test by dropping a little of the mixture on a plate to see whether it lifts off when cool.

Remove from heat and transfer to 5-quart electric mixer. Beat with paddle attachment until mixture forms a paste. Spread the paste evenly onto the square cake pan, taking care not to wrinkle the paper. Spread the paste evenly so that no air spaces form when it cools. After 24 hours the *ate* should be a solid cake of jelly. With a sharp knife, slice into 2 4-by-8-inch rectangles. Wrap in cellophane paper and store in airtight container until ready to serve. Slice as you would a block of cheese.

LIMONES GARAPIÑADOS
(Candied Limes)

These candied limes can be used to decorate cakes or to eat by themselves.

2 limes   **1½ cups water**
½ cup sugar

    Squeeze juice from limes and reserve in refrigerator for any later uses. Slice 2 lime peels thinly. In a heavy pan on high heat, boil sugar and water 3 minutes. Add lime peels. Reduce heat to medium and simmer 1 hour, or until skin is softened. Cool on wire rack set over cookie sheet. Dry on rack 12 hours. Refrigerate in a covered plastic container.

CHAPTER 20
BEVERAGES

''Fresh waters'' in Mexico does not refer to water that might run in a river, but rather to beverages prepared by cooking or soaking dried flowers, pods, or seeds in water and then adding sugar just before chilling.

AGUA DE JAMAICA
(Jamaica Water)

4 oz. dried Jamaica flowers   **Sugar to taste**
10 cups water

In a strainer under running water, rinse the Jamaica flowers. In a large pot, bring 10 cups water to a boil, mix in Jamaica flowers, reduce heat, and let simmer 3 minutes. Remove from stove and let stand at room temperature for 8 hours or overnight. Discard Jamaica flowers and mix in sugar to taste. Serve in tall glasses full of ice. Serves 6.

AGUA DE TAMARINDO
(Tamarind Water)

1 lb. tamarind pods   **Sugar to taste**
10 cups water

Peel and rinse the tamarind pods. Transfer them to a large pot, cover with 10 cups water, and let rest for 8 hours in a cool place. Add sugar to taste. Pour over tall glasses full of ice. Serves 6.

PONCHE FRÍO DE FRUTAS
(Cold Fruit Punch)

2 12-oz. bottles carbonated apple juice   **1 cup water**
2 12-oz. bottles carbonated mineral water   **1 cup sugar**
3 cups white wine   **4 cups watermelon, chopped**
          3 cups strawberries

Chill the carbonated apple juice, mineral water, and white wine.

In a small heavy saucepan, bring water and sugar to a boil, reduce heat, and simmer until it forms a syrup, about 5 minutes. Let come to room temperature.

Just before assembling the punch, chop the watermelon into bite-size chunks. Slice the strawberries.

In a punch bowl, mix the syrup with the chilled drinks, then add the fruit. Serve immediately with a little ice in each glass. Serves 6.

PONCHE CALIENTE DE FRUTAS
(Hot Fruit Punch)

This hot fruit punch is popular at the Christmas *posadas*. You will not be able to drive home after drinking it, but it is delicious. Better designate a driver for this one.

3 guavas
3 oranges
6 crab apples
1 piece sugarcane

¾ cup sugar
1 cup brandy
10 cups water
1 stick cinnamon

Chop guavas. Peel, seed, and cut oranges into pieces. Peel and chop the crab apples into small pieces. Peel and chop the sugarcane into ½-inch pieces.

In a dutch oven on low heat, cook the sugar and fruit until the sugar caramelizes and coats the fruit. Add the brandy, water, and cinnamon stick. Simmer for 15 minutes until the fruit is soft. Discard cinnamon stick. Serve hot in earthenware mugs.

Note: More brandy can be added, if desired. Serves 6.

CHOCOLATE A LA MEXICANA
(Mexican Hot Chocolate)

Traditionally, this recipe was made in an earthenware pot and stirred with a special wooden beater called a "molinillo". This recipe calls for an electric hand beater. Try to find the authentic Mexican chocolate tablets in your grocery store as they will preserve the cinnamon flavor.

3 squares sweetened Mexican
   chocolate

6 cups milk

In an earthenware pot on medium heat, warm the chocolate and the milk until the chocolate melts, stirring constantly. Bring to a boil and immediately remove from stove. Beat with a hand beater until a thick foam rises to the top. Serve immediately in earthenware mugs. Serves 6.

CAFÉ DE OLLA
(Coffee Made in an Earthenware Pot)

6 cups water
6 tsp. ground coffee
1 stick cinnamon

2 whole cloves
3 tbsp. piloncillo or brown sugar

In a large earthenware pot, boil all the ingredients for 5 to 8 minutes. Turn heat off and let grounds settle. Ladle into earthenware mugs. Serves 6.

ATOLE

Sweet tamales are generally accompanied by an earthenware mug of atole.

This is a basic recipe for preparing atole. If you want to make atole we recommend that you purchase a product at your grocery store called ''Maizena'' cornstarch, which is a product from Mexico that comes in chocolate, coconut, vanilla, cinnamon, almond, mango, guava, and pineapple flavors.

1 cup corn flour
½ cup rice flour
2 tbsp. cornstarch

8 cups water
Brown sugar or piloncillo, to taste

In a large heavy pot, mix flours and cornstarch. Mix in 2 cups water, stirring constantly until it becomes a smooth consistency. Transfer to stove and mix in remaining water. Bring to a boil, reduce heat to medium, and simmer until the mixture becomes thick. Mix in brown sugar or piloncillo to taste. Serve in earthenware mugs. Serves 6.

Glossary

For some non-Latins, as well as Latin Americans who have never been in Mexico, certain terms in Mexican cooking will be unfamiliar to you, so here we provide you with a brief reference guide to the more common ones.

Mexico	Other Latin Countries	U.S.A.
aceite	aceite	oil
aceituna	aceituna	olive
achiote	achiote	annatto (pulp of annatto tree)
aguacate	palta	avocado
ajo	ajo	garlic
ajonjoli	ajonjoli	sesame seed
albahaca	albahaca	basil
almendra	almendra	almond
anís	anís	anise
arroz	arroz	rice
azafrán	azafrán	saffron
azúcar	azúcar	sugar
betabel	beterraga, remolacha	beet
bolillo	marraqueta	French roll
cacahuate	maní	peanut
cal	cal	lime (oxide of calcium)
calabaza	zapallo	squash (or pumpkin)
camarón	camarón	shrimp
camote	camote	sweet potato
canela	canela	cinnamon

cazuela	*cazuela*	casserole
cebada	*cebada*	barley
cebolla	*cebolla*	onion
chícharos	*arvejas*	peas
chile	*ají*	chili
cilantro	*culantro*	coriander
clavo de olor	*clavo de olor*	clove
coco	*coco*	coconut
col	*repollo*	cabbage
comal	*comal*	griddle
comino	*comino*	cumin
ejotes	*judías*	string beans
elotes	*choclos*	corn
eneldo	*eneldo*	dill
fideos	*fideos*	vermicelli
filete migon	*lomo*	filet mignon
fríjoles	*porotos,*	beans
	habichuelas	
glucosa	*glucosa*	corn syrup
guajolote	*pavo*	turkey
guayaba	*guayaba*	guava
harina	*harina*	flour
helado	*helado*	ice cream
hinojo	*hinojo*	fennel
huachinango	*huachinango*	red snapper
huevo	*huevo*	egg
jaiba	*cangrejo*	crab
jamón	*jamón*	ham
jarabe	*jarabe*	syrup
jarros	*jarros*	pitchers
jitomate	*tomate*	tomato
jugo	*jugo*	juice
laurel	*laurel*	bay leaf
leche	*leche*	milk
lechuga	*lechuga*	lettuce
lenteja	*lenteja*	lentil
levadura	*levadura*	yeast
limón	*limón*	lime
lomo de puerco	*lomo de puerco*	pork loin
maíz	*maíz*	maize

maizena	fécula de maíz	cornstarch
manteca	manteca	lard
manzana	manzana	apple
masa	masa	dough
moscabado	mascabada	brown sugar
mejorana	mejorana	marjoram
melón	melón	cantaloupe
membrillo	membrillo	quince
migajas	migas	crumbs
migajón	migas de pan	soft inside of bread
mostaza	mostaza	mustard
nabo	nabo	turnip
naranja	naranja	orange
nuez moscada	nuez moscada	nutmeg
olla	olla	pots
palillo	palillo	toothpick
pan	pan	bread
papel	papel	paper
pasa	pasa	raisin
pastel	torta	cake
pavo	pavo	turkey
pepino	pepino	cucumber
pera	pera	pear
pescado	pescado	fish
piloncillo	azúcar de pilón	unrefined sugar loaf (or brown sugar)
piña	ananá	pineapple
piñón	piñón	pine nut
plátano	plátano	banana
plátano macho	plátano de cocinar	plantain (banana not a substitute)
pollo	pollo	chicken
pozole	motes	hominy
puerco	puerco, chancho	pig
puerro	poro	leek
rábano	rábano	radish
relleno	relleno	stuffing
res	res	beef

róbalo	*róbalo*	bass
romero	*romero*	rosemary
salchicha	*salchicha*	sausage
salvia	*salvia*	sage
sandía	*sandía*	watermelon
semilla	*semilla*	seed
sopa	*sopa*	soup
tamarindo	*tamarindo*	tamarind
telera	*marraqueta*	french roll
tocino	*tocino*	bacon
tomillo	*tomillo*	thyme
torta	*sandwich*	hero sandwich
tortilla española	*tortilla*	egg omelet
trucha	*trucha*	trout
uvas	*uvas*	grapes
verduras	*verduras*	vegetables
vinagre	*vinagre*	vinegar
vino	*vino*	wine
yema	*yema*	yolk
yerba	*yerba*	herb
zanahoria	*zanahoria*	carrot

Index

Índice